A BASEBALL BIRTHRIGHT

Copyright © 2022 by Pasquale A. Carlucci

All rights reserved. No part of this publication may be reproduced, stored in a retrieval system, distributed or transmitted in any form or by any means, electronic, mechanical, photocopying, recording or otherwise, without the prior written permission of the author, except by a reviewer who may quote brief passages in a review.

For permission requests or more information contact:

Pat Carlucci
611 Pennsylvania Avenue SE #340
Washington, DC 20003

pat@baseballbirthright.com
www.baseballbirthright.com

979-8-88759-093-6 paperback
979-8-88759-145-2 hardback
979-8-88759-094-3 ebook

A BASEBALL BIRTHRIGHT

CHRONICLES & CONNECTIONS

PASQUALE A. CARLUCCI

For Carmen, Wynn and Lila and
in loving memory of John and Beatrice Carlucci

CONTENTS

INTRODUCTION — 1

CHAPTER 1 — 3
Raincheck - An Explanation

CHAPTER 2 — 19
Batting Practice - A Birth and A Shot

CHAPTER 3 — 37
1st Inning - "Joltin Joe" & the "Kid"

CHAPTER 4 — 45
2nd Inning - Bronx Bedlam

CHAPTER 5 — 59
3rd Inning - A Funeral and a Rose

CHAPTER 6 — 65
4th Inning - Royal Pain

CHAPTER 7 — 73
5th Inning - Tiger Town

CHAPTER 8 — 87
6th Inning - Battle of the Blimps

CHAPTER 9 — 99
7th Inning - New York Minute

CHAPTER 10 — 113
8th Inning - Triboro Toll

CHAPTER 11 — 121
9th Inning - "Ya Gotta Believe!"

CHAPTER 12 — 137
Clubhouse - Bored in Boston

CHAPTER 13 — 147
Bench - Century's Pre-Game

CHAPTER 14 — 159
Bullpen - Perfect Perch

CHAPTER 15 — 167
The Showers - Father's Day "Gift"

CHAPTER 16 — 177
Grandstands - Baseball BOGO

AFTER-FORWARD — 189

ACKNOWLEDGMENTS — 197

BIBLIOGRAPHY — 203

INTRODUCTION

I'm 70 years old and I'm a fan of baseball.

Seventy is a nice round number and also is the age which I hit halfway through the completion of this project. This book is about baseball. Numbers matter.

I consider myself to be the luckiest man on the face of the earth. If this statement does not ring your bell, yet you claim to be an avid baseball fan, it may mean that you are still young (if so, Google: Lou Gehrig, player, 1936, or Gary Cooper, actor, 1946).

I have been fortunate enough to have had a diversified business career, one rich in disparate companies and assorted geographies, but this book is mostly about my luck with the game of baseball.

This is a collection of stories about great games which I luckily have witnessed over a 60-year period. I was never alone on this journey. Friends, family, and business colleagues accompanied me along the way. This compilation also serves as a set of life stories traced through the lens of America's pastime.

The baseball fanatic will love it. The casual sports fan should enjoy it. Since it recounts contemporary

American history, sprinkled with a measure of business elements, there is something for nearly everyone—the sports fan, the history buff, the biography enthusiast, the beach vacationer.

I did learn through this process that my memory is visual—no, *very* visual—while my attention to specific details (such as names, places, and the like) is less so. I enlisted help in recreating the events from friends, family, business colleagues, and, thankfully, the internet. I have done my best to get the facts correct, especially the numbers. You could even call me a perfectionist. Yet I'm not perfect.

I hope that you enjoy reading it as much as I relished producing it.

I also wish that it rekindles great memories for you from your lifetime, no matter your age. Take it from this senior citizen and lucky grandfather: the days seem like minutes, but the memories last forever.

CHAPTER 1

RAINCHECK - AN EXPLANATION

I enjoy watching and following most any type of sport. I especially like those played with a ball, though that ball may be of any shape, and the sport may take place at any time of year, professional, collegiate or otherwise. But above anything else, I love professional baseball.

For more than half a century, I have been fortunate to attend scores of Major League Baseball games in various cities across the country. Many of the games were unexpected, and a number have been historic —way beyond any one fan's fair share. I often happen to be at the right place at the right time.

The games have been awesome. Their stories, sometimes amazing. I was considering drafting an article about this last point when a friend suggested a book. So, here you and I are.

At first, the idea of authoring a book was certainly daunting. I had never attempted such an assignment. A summer book report, yes; a blue book in a college final examination, yes; a master's thesis for a graduate degree, yes; a book, nope. The thought had never before crossed my mind, but my notions of intimidation all occurred pre-pandemic. Post-pandemic, my feelings toward authorship had shifted. Daunting? Not any longer. A commitment? Assumed and discovered. Entertaining? Hopefully—and, hopefully, not just for me.

The pandemic environment was the stimulus, as it was for thousands of others—and why not? Everyone was looking to escape. There was so much information, or lack thereof, to process—general chaos, life prioritization, family protection planning, daily adjustment, contact tracing, hand sanitizing, no Clorox, no Charmin, asymptomatic, no face touching, facemasks, Facetime, lockdown, layoffs, resignations; an endless alphabetization of media, bureaucracy, and stimulus—CDC, CNN, WHO, FOX, NIH, SBA, FDA, PPP, CARES, EIDLP; clinical studies, essential workers, PPE, N95 masks, quarantines, school shutdowns, remote learning, class in the park, virtual cocktails, relief loans, ventilators, ventilation systems, remote workplace, workplace safety, privacy, individual rights, UPS, FEDEX, USPS, home delivery, curbside pickup, sidewalk dining, new normal, Zoom, Phase Two, webinars, the clock, Twitter, Tik-Tok, PCR testing, vaccinations, re-openings, closings,

CHAPTER 1

funerals, bankruptcy, Phase Three, QR codes, social distancing, pods, podcasts, vaccines, social unrest, politicization, hybrid, boosters, inflation —

Wait! What? Social Distancing? Now *that* struck a chord. More than ever, people realized they wanted to be with other people—with almost anybody, in fact. With family, in an office, in supermarket aisles, in a bowling alley, in a movie theater, a bar, a restaurant, a park, a zoo, inside a mall, or **at a baseball game.**

I originally thought a recounting of my many special game experiences would be a great read for the avid baseball fan. The casual sports fan might, too, enjoy the narrative. Readers may be interested in business, sales, consulting, or even history. There would be a little something for everyone. Then again, now I have realized that this book might be right for *anyone* looking for that escape, whether they be at the beach or in quarantine. I would be more than okay if one hundred percent of this book's readership was comprised of family and friends. I must say that I am curious to find out.

Now this excited me, even made me dizzy—admittedly a state not difficult to achieve when quarantined with three rescued canines in a small row house. I concluded that the writing needed to focus on more than the great games, their unfolding drama, or the magical hits.

The social distancing protocol spotlighted baseball's innate and distinct quality, the reason why it is so unique. Baseball is not only the nation's past-time; baseball is an enjoyable way to pass the time. Plain and simple. Family, community, memories, diversity, history, childhood, constancy, entertainment, timelessness—they are all there, instantly, when you enter a major league ballpark, whether for the first time or the one-hundredth time.

Sharing a conversation with a dad, a customer, a friend, a neighbor, a child, a son, a daughter, a grandson, a granddaughter, a first-time witness, a Little Leaguer, a client, a stranger, and all the rest and the very many about baseball create *connections*, instantaneously—maybe for a minute, for an out, for an inning, for a doubleheader, or forever. This is not because of the game, but because of being at the game, and with whom and why. If the game turned out to be special, all the better. Either way, baseball kindles great memories

My personal attraction to baseball is its complexity. How can such a simple sport be so multidimensional? The beauty is in the eye of the beholder. For me, it has been engaging for a lifetime. The draw includes many aspects, and it literally has no limitations.

Here is just a start, with illustrations: mathematical (batting average, ninety feet, sabermetrics), generational (Ty Cobb, Joe DiMaggio, Cal Ripken, Mike Trout, Jacob DeGrom), team (New York Highlanders, Brooklyn Dodgers, New York Mets), individual (Ted Williams, Pete Rose, Pete Alonzo), competition (the

Most Valuable Player, the standings, the World Series), peak performance (a home run, the batting title, the Cy Young Award, the Triple Crown), greatness (Stan Musial, Warren Spahn, Willie Mays), rules (the balk, the lineup card, the designated hitter), judgement calls (a strike, an error, the foul pole), storytelling (Babe Ruth), history (the Negro Leagues, Jackie Robinson, Satchel Paige, Frank Robinson), reverence (Cooperstown), the soiled side (Shoeless Joe Jackson and the Black Sox, Barry Bonds and steroids abuse, the cheating world champion Houston Astros), courage (Lou Gehrig, Jackie Robinson, Roberto Clemente, Hank Aaron), drama (the perfect game, Bobby Thompson, Bill Mazeroski, Bill Buckner with Mookie Wilson, Joe Carter, the walk-off win), tradition (Wrigley Field, the seventh inning stretch, Fenway Park), entertainment (Bill Veeck, the All-Star Game, the Home Run Derby, extra innings), statistics (56, 714, 60, .406), business (the players union, television contracts, the reserve clause, the abbreviated pandemic season), rivalries (Red Sox–Yankees, Dodgers–Giants, Mets–Braves), strategy (the bullpen, the bunt, the pinch hitter), personalities (Leo Durocher, Yogi Berra, Reggie Jackson, Rickey Henderson, Juan Soto), and so much more.

On top of all of that, like no other American sport, baseball offers us a unique mirror of American culture, a reflection of American society—the good, the bad, and the ugly—since the turn of two centuries.

Particularly favorite perspectives for me are the clock, the game, the guarantee, the math, and the season:

The clock: there is none. The game's end is up to that day's players and their competition; twenty-seven outs each, at least.

The game: a simple game, but a complex sport. Ball, bat, glove; pitch, hit, field—but ah, the rules.

The guarantee: you will see something on the field which has never happened before—or, in the least, which *you* have never seen before.

The math: numerical analysis, linear algebra, statistics. (I enjoyed mathematics and received good grades—though I did hit the wall with calculus.)

The season: it is long. 162 games, six months; a marathon for the players, a game every day for the fans. You do not have to wait until Sunday for the next game.

One of my generation's greatest comedians, George Carlin[1], routinely performed a bit called *Football and*

---

[1] Carlin performed decades of hilarious and diverse standup routines. George was indeed one of a kind with a great mind, and a

CHAPTER 1

Baseball. As host of NBC's *Saturday Night Live's (SNL)* very first episode, on October 11, 1975, the artist sauntered down from the audience balcony to the live stage to present the differences between the two sports. Carlin describes baseball as a "nineteenth century pastoral game," while football is a "twentieth century technological game," and then takes off from there. The act resonates so well that even today, nearly fifty years later, visitors (especially kids) sit, watch, and laugh at its video replay in the Baseball Hall of Fame Museum in Cooperstown, New York.

As I interviewed those who accompanied (connections) me to these special games (chronicles) decades ago, I began to realize a common response: discussion of the game—or just baseball in general—conjured up lifetime memories for them, memories that were much more important than the scores and stats. The games were signposts acting as catalysts for the recall of rich memories, many beyond baseball—an intersection of life and sport.

This book is a compilation of short game stories. This is not the author's intention, but the reader may view it as a memoir or a biography. If so, so be it, but

---

high school dropout. (If he had graduated, it would have been from my high school and alma mater in the south Bronx. After his first year, he was either tossed or walked out. I am guessing that it was the latter since he never received a high school diploma—ah, the rules.)

regardless, the form is only a vehicle with which to tell a fortunate journey. Therein lies the true story.

THE BASEBALL GODS

The circumstances recounted here are personally meaningful to me. When viewed separately, the reader may legitimately construe the events as interesting also, but meaningless. However, when considered as a whole, they could (really, *should*) give the reader pause. The reader may find themselves thinking, how could this one fan be at all these great games? The writer does not work for Major League Baseball or for the New York Mets, is not a television camera operator or a sports journalist or newspaper sportswriter. Surely, he is not a best-selling author.

The pause might lead to a thought, possibly a question, leading to a hypothesis.

For instance: do baseball gods exist? I was surprised to discover that there are numerous books and articles authored on this subject. If so, is their purpose to oversee only the teams, players, managers, coaches, cities, owners, traditions, records, union, and the league? Or do baseball fans fall within the purview of their job description? If so, is it for all fans or just for a select few—or maybe even just for one, earmarked by the day of his birth, as flaky as it may sound?

I have developed my own opinion. Feel free to read on and choose to agree or disagree.

CHAPTER 1

I will admit that there is another driving catalyst for this project. Not too long ago, I wondered, what could be worse than Major League Baseball's handling and bungling of the Astros' sign cheating scandal in Houston? A global pandemic and a year without baseball qualifies; for one thing, we were cheated out of watching and tracking how many times the Astros were hit by pitched balls (HPB) over the course of a full 162 game season. You absolutely knew that it was coming. Covid cheated me out of charting the cheaters.

But then it did worsen: a global pandemic *with* baseball. This worsened it on so many levels: the wrong moral decision, the risk to the players and families, the owners' grab for the money, and I guess the players too.

At that exact point in time—July 23, 2020—I decided to boycott, to go on strike. I was determined not to watch, listen, read, or follow any of the 2020 Major League Baseball "season." I would substitute all this time I annually focused on baseball (which was a lot) by writing about it, instead. I can attest truthfully here that I held to this word. I did not view a single pitch of the eventual sixty-game "season," or its meaningless conclusion, the COVID SERIES. (Who won, anyway?) Simply stated, I opted out of the season (similar to a few intelligent players) without an agent, choosing to write this instead.

MY START WITH BASEBALL

My parents, John and Beatrice Carlucci, are first-generation Americans, children of immigrant parents, courtesy of Ellis Island. They grew up fast as a part of America's Greatest Generation, raised during the Great Depression. As both were born in Brooklyn, mom and dad were Dodger fans naturally, but not automatically. Yankee fans also resided in this borough.

John was one of eight children and was an eventually recognized veteran of World War II—a Merchant Marine serving as his ship's purser and nurse. (There is a story that on his first mission, he became so seasick for so long that when he returned headed back to Brooklyn, he went AWOL; the story ends quickly with my grandmother kicking his butt back to his ship in Boston.) With his feet finally planted on solid ground, he followed this up with a lengthy career as a bookkeeper and office manager for a family-owned coffee company in Yonkers, New York.

Beatrice was one of nine and born on Veterans Day. She had the harder job: she was mother to four.

After the Bums (DBA Brooklyn Dodgers) relocated to California in 1958, my parents were no longer rabid baseball fans. Dad golfed. Mom was mother to four.

My affinity for baseball was automatic, as it was for most kids. My affinity for the National League is genetically wired. You can say the same about my affinity for my favorite team, the New York Mets—although they were born after me.

I am a Baby Boomer (AKA the luckiest generation) and graduated high school in the late sixties. These were turbulent times, and not just because it was the first time I could legally lift a beer (accompanied by beer nuts—sometimes pretzels, if the former were out of stock—and usually in an establishment known as the Greenleaf). We, like our parents, also grew up fast: protests, Vietnam, riots, cities burning, blackouts, assassinations, moon landing, Woodstock, the Miracle Mets, and all the rest.

I write we are the *luckiest* generation because we had the chance to work for a company for life or for a long while, incur no lasting college loan debt, eventually were able to own a house, accrue some retirement money, and, if lucky and careful, live long enough to enjoy grandchildren. This employment aspect has much to do with the situations and circumstances which lead to these *chronicles* and *connections*.

To be clear here at the beginning: my belief is that my numerous, special major league baseball experiences are not a result of luck or coincidence. They are rather due to a predestined path set in motion by the specific day of my birth. As far-fetched as that may read, this is not fiction. Along the way, special situations facilitated my personal passage through baseball. My business career, for instance, was accommodating—if not, downright delineating. Four separate callings with four differing companies defined my course:

- The public company General Foods Corporation (later Kraft Foods) marketed to its key accounts, distributors, and consumers.
- The self-owned consulting firm, LC&A, had its industry share groups, clients, and partners.
- The family-owned food company, Country Home Bakers, collaborated with its customers, trade associations, and sales partners.
- The private firm, Allen Austin, has its partners, clients, and candidates.

These four distinctly distinct cultures had two things in common. The first was that my job with each of them required quite a bit of business travel. Individually, one may have been operating out of a remote, regional, or corporate office. The accounts, customers, and clients were located where they were located, and business was conducted on a maskless, face-to- face basis.

The second alike aspect was the entertainment of these same groups, which spanned most sports and venues. I suffered the personal hardship of catering to key customers while multitasking, enjoying championship competitions such as: NFL Super Bowls (XVI, XXXV), NCAA College Basketball - Final Fours (1988, 2000), US Open Tennis Championships, World Olym-

CHAPTER 1

pics (Calgary 1988), NBA, NHL, and NCAA College Football games, the Kentucky Derby, NASCAR (Daytona), LPGA, and PGA (US Open, Pebble Beach).

All of these experiences were great. Most were fantastic. A few were exciting and dramatic. None of them were baseball.

Season tickets were sometimes a part of the company's sales entertainment or customer development budget. There was no bigger bang for the buck than Major League Baseball. It was mathematical. There are eighty-one home games in the season. Occasionally (and hopefully) the season would be prolonged. The ticket package would stake further claim to postseason games—that is, if the home team played well enough long enough (or became lucky enough) to achieve that level of success. That is the point of playing all of the 162 games, come rain or eventual shine.

I was lucky over the years, because of my position and positions. I had access to a number of these season ticket plans, though all were partial plans—usually no more than twenty games per season. My specific involvement included the Kansas City Royals (1980, 1981), the Detroit Tigers (1982, 1983, 1984), the New York Mets (2000, 2001, 2002) and the Washington Nationals (2018, 2019).

Our family's moves and a half century journey of corporate relocations offered chances to experience and see unfamiliar places. In fact, the facts and history

A BASEBALL BIRTHRIGHT

show that our residential whereabouts may have been influential in my baseball journey. Maybe it was just luck or coincidence, but that argument is not likely. It is undeniable: the baseball relocation gods were at work.

In eight of nine instances, following my change in address, that new city's team would make it all the way to the World Series within the next one or two (one time, it was three) years. Two of the franchises achieved this accomplishment for the first time in team history. The only team that did not make it to the World Series shattered team hitting records that year, instead. A perfect score of nine of nine, 100 percent, is the mark of my "influence":

1951	Womb to Queens	1951	New York Giants	Loser
1955	Queens to Yonkers	1955	Brooklyn Dodgers	Winner
1974	Yonkers to Queens	1976	New York Yankees	Loser
1976	Queens to Chicago	1977	Chicago White Sox[2]	------
1977	Chicago to Queens	1978	New York Yankees	Winner
1980	Queens to Kansas	1980	Kansas City Royals+[3]	Loser
1981	Kansas to Michigan	1984	Detroit Tigers	Winner
1984	Michigan to NY/CT	1986	New York Mets	Winner
2017	NY/CT to Washington, DC	2019	Washington Nationals[4]	Winner

Is 100 percent a coincidence? Possibly. Is it factual? Definitely. Is my theory delusional? Maybe, but there is

---

[2] Most Hits, Most Home Runs, Most RBI's & Highest Batting Average in franchise history.

[3] First World Series appearance in franchise history

[4] First World Series appearance in franchise history

just too much baseball stuff associated with my life to cry "coincidence." Baseball was born in New York and so was I, and not just on an ordinary day, but on the day of the most famous play in sports history. That is how I care to see it.

THE PROCESS

Chapters are entitled "innings." Similar to a game completed in regulation, they follow from 1 to 9 and are sequential. But then there was a need to stop and adjust. There were just too many great games to recount. We would be going into extra, extra innings—for a very long time.

Part of the research employed here was to recall and select the best games I have seen (frankly, there are just too many to include all of them), and then develop their *chronicle*. In each case and for every game, the author contacted and interviewed the *connection* who joined him. These *connections* have never forgotten the day. To my delight, their rich memories have enhanced the process of my writing, and—I sensed—in a small way, their lives.

CHAPTER 2

BATTING PRACTICE - A BIRTH AND A SHOT

October 3, 1951

I found this first chapter to be the most challenging to write, and not just because it is the first one. I possess no personal recollection of this iconic game played in New York City. You would think I should. The game, which was nationally televised (a rarity at the time), was globally radio-broadcast to reach the many active military outposts and stations around the world at that time. *The Miracle of Coogan's Bluff* is arguably the most famous game in baseball history, and there would be truly little arguing about it. The game concluded with *The Shot Heard 'Round the World*—literally.

This seems like a natural place to start. I was unable to watch it, and incapable to attend. I was in a hospital with my mother. I was being born.

I do recollect my first World Series. In the fall of 1959, I was enjoying the games on our first RCA color television, which was really a large piece of furniture. The cinematography was black and white, as my memory is fuzzy and gray. I watched from my usual position, lying on the floor, usually a great front row seat in our family's cozy (read: small) "TV Room."

The Dodgers, who had recently relocated and now represented the city of Los Angeles, faced off against the Chicago White Sox. This was the first appearance for Chicago in forty years, the first since the White Sox were black. (The Black Sox Scandal was a Major League Baseball game- fixing scandal. Eight members of the White Sox were accused of throwing the 1919 World Series against the Cincinnati Reds in exchange for money from a gambling syndicate. The great American pastime almost did not recover.)

The Bums, no longer a Brooklyn fan's endearment, eventually prevailed. The Los Angeles club marked its first championship in Hollywood, the first in history for a west coast team. The victory was accomplished in six games, the winning margin 4-2. Somehow, I recall the competition being closer.

The Dodgers had a great lineup, plus the Hall of Fame pitching duo of Sandy Koufax and Don Drysdale. As it often turns out on the biggest of stages, not the biggest star makes the biggest impact. This especially seems to be the case in the sport of baseball. Despite the two just mentioned, a pedestrian pitcher named

CHAPTER 2

Larry Sherry was voted Most Valuable Player (MVP) of the World Series. Sherry earned it, figuring in all four Dodger wins—winning two and saving two others. The performance must have been quite a thrill for him. Sherry was home-grown, a local Los Angeles product. 1959 was his first full year in the major leagues and the MVP award was a well-deserved legacy. The "Go-Go White Sox" were gone.

When I reached back to review this game now, I realized I had no idea of the greatness I was watching then. Besides Koufax and Drysdale, Dodger players included Gil Hodges, John Roseboro, Duke Snyder, Carl Furillo, Junior (Jim) Gilliam, Maury Wills, and Roger Craig. Chicago fielded Early Wynn, Luis Aparicio, Ted Kluszenski, and Nellie Fox. The opposing managers were Walter Alston and Al Lopez. I might be miscounting, but there were at least nine members of baseball's Hall of Fame playing in the series—not to mention a White Sox outfielder nicknamed "Jungle Jim" Rivera. If absolutely none of the above names seem familiar, you might want to stop reading or maybe appreciate that you are still young.

Within the confines of my intimate Washington, DC, garage, there exists a mini baseball archive, a collection of sorts, which is personal, if not collectable. Included are scorecards, programs, photographs, posters, memorabilia, trading cards, autographed balls, coffee mugs, and beer glasses. There are not too many of each—except the cards, which span three decades. Most of these are from the sixties. One of the "year collection" sets recorded each game with a special World Series card. This particular year seems to be the last set printed horizontally (landscape), not vertically (portrait). I prefer that format. I do not think that it ever came back into style, but I have not researched it.

My 1960 collection is a copious one probably because it was my first. Koufax, Drysdale, and Sherry are all present and accounted for, as are numerous doubles, triples, and extras. The cards are unquestionably not in mint condition and are rather tattered, but were mercifully rescued from their original shoebox. Similar to many of the players which they depicted, the collection has character, but show the wear and tear of being regularly flipped in the lunch-time schoolyard.

These World Series Dodgers come to mind because, as an eight-year-old, I understood that the Fall Classic marked the end of baseball's "school year." Grades were public. The team class rank is posted. Unlike the student and the academic school year, the baseball fan is oblivious to the actual calendar. Spring does not appear until Opening Day. Autumn is marked by the start of the World Series. Baseball's marquis event is the culmination and pinnacle of a six-month-long pilgrimage of both player and fan.

In the beginning—or, at least, in 1951—a full regular season consisted of 154 games (162 was enacted in

1961, confirmed by one of the cruelest asterisks which marked—and demeaned—the accomplishment of New York Yankee Roger Maris when he broke Babe Ruth's single season record for most home runs: 61 in '61. You can usually count on Major League Baseball to do the wrong thing).

Occasionally back then, in a rare season, baseball treated fans to a few extra, bonus games. These would be when a "playoff" might be required to determine a league champion. Like in 1951.

Times were much simpler then. So was baseball. There were two leagues: the National and the American. Each had eight teams. Each team played each of the other teams within their own league a total twenty-two times: 7 opponents x 22 games = 154 games. Simple, organized, symmetrical. Yet, in the end, it could still get complicated. If two or more teams finished the regular season standings in a tie, a playoff game and/or a playoff series would determine the top of the class. For the longest time, this was known as winning the "pennant." Today, you do not really hear that phrase any longer. Back then, it meant everything.

In this year (1951), there was to be a "best of three games" playoff series to determine a winner. The two National League clubs in New York finished the regular season tied with the same record, 96 wins and 58 losses. The New York Giants unexpectedly had propelled this situation by their scorching-hot finish in August and

September, the final two months of the season. The Giants had won 16 consecutive games in August and caught up with the Dodgers.[1]

The Giants of Manhattan were to square off in a winner-take-all confrontation with the Dodgers of Brooklyn for the right to play the New York Yankees of the Bronx in the World Series. The Yanks were Champions of the American League again, and as usual.

The inescapable irony is not lost on me: an immortal playoff game occurred on the day of my birth, and it coincides here with the modern-day cheating scandal of the 2017 Houston Astros. That later affair was likely repeated in 2016 and 2018, two years never to be really known because of the whitewashing partnership of Major League Baseball and the Major League Baseball's Players Association. As previously mentioned, you can count on MLB to do the wrong thing.

If you were lucky enough to attend a World Series game during the fifties, you were almost always in

---

[1] Throughout the league it was commonly known that the Giants were probably stealing opposing catchers' signs relayed to the bullpen. The system used a strategically positioned telescope inside the manager's office located above centerfield. Leo Durocher was the Giant manager, the same Leo of "nice guys finish last" fame. Leo the Lip devised the spying system. For intricate detail of the scheme and insight of the lifelong drama of the two key players, I refer the reader to Joshua's Prager's *The Echoing Green, The Untold Story of Bobby Thomson, Ralph Branca And The Shot Heard Round The World*.

the Big Apple—at a stadium in one of three boroughs. Often, you might be traveling between two. The documentary miniseries, *Baseball,* created by Ken Burns and originally aired on the Public Broadcasting Station (PBS) in 1994, covered the greatness of the three New York teams. Interest was national, but the focus was usually local. The series titled the segment, "The Capital of Baseball."

This Golden Age of Baseball was unlike anything seen in any sport today. The teams were much more than professional baseball clubs—they represented neighborhoods and communities of New York City. Most players remained with the teams which discovered and developed them, and which eventually brought them up into the big leagues.

(Although, the owners did have 100 percent control of player contracts, because of baseball's reserve clause. The teams prohibited any player who refused a contract from playing for any other professional team until 1975.)

Players lived within the community, along with their fans. Like everyone else in the neighborhood, they had a day job, went to church or synagogue, had side jobs, shopped in stores and open markets, dined in restaurants. The daily newspaper recorded their job performance and grades. As a result, the players often heard about it from their teachers, fans, and neighbors—one way or the other.

A BASEBALL BIRTHRIGHT

The 1951 National League playoff series was a war between two communities.

Bill Madden, in his important baseball book, *1954: The Year Willie Mays and the First Generation of Black Superstars Changed Major League Baseball Forever*, writes specifically about one New York borough:

"...Brooklyn, the largest of the five boroughs, with a population of 2.7 million, more than any other city in the United States except Chicago and Los Angeles. Dodger fans were like no others, ingrained as they were with the pathos of having never experienced a world championship banner hoisted up the flagpole in Ebbets Field. Theirs was a love-hate relationship, in which they embraced their heroes like family—a lot of the Dodgers lived right there among them in the neighborhoods—but would lovingly disparage the "bums" when they lost. Brooklyn's was largely a blue-collar populace comprised of Italian, Irish, Asian, and Jewish immigrants along with the heaviest concentration of black citizens in the United States."

Dad and Mom were born and raised in Brooklyn. John (Giovanni) lived on Montrose Avenue in the Williamsburg section, while Beatrice (Pietrina) lived on Gates Avenue in the neighboring Bushwick section. My parents were introduced to each other by Dad's older brother, Emil, and Mom's older sister, Joan (the two also wed each other). Mom graduated from Bushwick High School, Dad from Eastern District High School.

The latter no longer exists, but did get its name when Williamsburg and Bushwick were annexed by the city of Brooklyn as its Eastern District in 1855.

Dad lived closest to Manhattan, near the Williamsburg Bridge. One of his many jobs was at the famed Fulton Fish Market at South Street Seaport near New York's financial district and by the Brooklyn Bridge on the East River. Dad would never have a tough time finding a seat on the subway ride back to Brooklyn, since the market's distinctive aroma accompanied him. I can only think that this job was pre-Mom.

My ten-year younger sister, Frances, is an executive with the Bank of New York, and she has been successfully employed there for her entire career. (This book has labored so long that she is actually now retiring, early). At one point she worked in offices located at One Wall Street. Dad also had another job, as a messenger in the financial district. Fran reminded me that Dad would regularly enjoy his spring or summertime lunch on Alexander Hamilton's grave in Trinity Cemetery. In addition to being a founding father of the United States, Hamilton founded the Bank of New York.

After marrying in 1949, my parents settled in South Ozone Park, Queens, a different borough and county but still minutes away from Brooklyn. For all of my adult life, I had assumed that my father sat uncomfortably in the Polo Grounds at this historic game, nearly staying long enough to personally witness the game's fateful ending. I am in possession of an original newspaper from Wednesday October 3, 1951. The morning edition of *The New York Times* showcased on its front page a photo of five smiling Dodgers with this accompanying heading: "SOME OF BIG GUNS IN DODGERS' ANSWERING SALVO."

World War II had just passed. The Korean War was in progress. Readers might have welcomed a less militaristic caption, but the point might have resonated less. The teams had knotted up the series at one game apiece. The Giants had won the opener. The Dodgers responded with their salvo. That left just one game to go to get to the World Series.

I have shared a tale of my dad's fateful baseball day at many a business cocktail hour. I would usually and eventually get a laugh, as well as a test of my listener's baseball historical acumen. "Guess my birth date, hint, hint?" That would be the first hurdle. Polite listeners would then have to bear the description of my dad's day—how the Polo Grounds office got *the call*, found him in his seat, and how he abruptly exited; how he had, somewhat comfortably even for a Dodgers fan, headed out to Memorial Hospital in Jamaica, Queens, to meet me for the first time.

Dad's Dodgers had just scored three runs in the top of the eighth inning to pull ahead 4 to 1. The Ace of their pitching staff, Don Newcomb (20 Wins–9 Losses in the regular season) was still in the game. (Just five years later, "Big Don" would become baseball's first Cy Young Award Winner as well as the National League's Most Valuable Player, in that same year).

Upon Dad's departure, the Giants started to peck away at Newcomb, promptly scoring a run in the bottom of their last and ninth inning. This started off with back-to-back, ground ball singles produced by the bats of Alvin Dark and Don Mueller. Monte Irwin flied out. Then Whitey Lockman's left field double scored Dark. Score now: Dodgers up 4–2. The Giants were getting closer in their final at bat.

For Brooklyn fans, it was becoming eerily and familiarly dark. Brooklyn fans were never immune to the expectation of their favorite team somehow finding a way to lose. (In this way, they are kindred spirits with lifelong NY Mets fans, likely via DNA and zip code.)

There were still two outs to go, still two runners on base, and still two hitters to bat. In clear sight was Bobby Thomson, the "Staten Island Scotsman" (born abroad, raised in a fifth NYC borough) walking up to the batter's box. Just as clear was a rookie by the name of Willie Mays, kneeling on one knee in the on-deck circle, in his first year in the majors. (The destiny of Mays is to become the greatest player ever to play the game. On this particular day, Willie had absolutely no desire to be the last at bat, or to make the last out.)

On the previous play there had been a devastating injury to Mueller, occurring on his slide into third base.

Players eventually carried him off the field on a stretcher. This long lull in the action only heightened the tension, extending the game's final moment. In the interim, the Dodgers decided to make a pitching change.

Manager Chuck (sometimes Charlie) Dressen sauntered to Big Don's pitching mound – which had been his for eight-and-one-third innings. Dressen signaled out to the bullpen to make a switch, summoning Ralph Branca, who now entered the game—and the moment. Branca was a three-time All Star (1947–1949) and in 1947 he posted 21 wins and a 2.67 ERA. The tall (6'3") and young (25 years old) fireballer was raised in Mount Vernon, New York.

Destined to be forever second-guessing, uneasy Dodgers fans wondered, why this move? And why now? Branca was a starter who barely pitched to .500 during the season (13–11); he did save three games, but he had blown three others. Then there was the fact that he was the losing pitcher in the first playoff game, which was still fresh in everyone's mind, as it had happened, just forty-eight hours earlier. Branca had given up just three runs in the 3–1 loss, all three runs surrendered via the long ball. The first home run was by Monte Irwin. The second—and deciding—one was a two-run homer by the current batter, Bobby Thomson.

Branca also wore a uniform with the number 13 on its back.

As my cocktail story goes, on his way to the hospital, Dad looked upon a storefront television just in time to witness it. Thompson tomahawked the second pitch thrown his way, depositing his eternal three-run home run shot a few rows over the left-field wall, just above the watchful, stunned eyes of Dodger left fielder, Andy Pafko. The Giants Win 5-4 and, of course, millions heard the excited announcer, Russ Hodges, immortalize the event: *"...The Giants Win the Pennant! The Giants Win the Pennant! The Giants Win the Pennant!"*

The pandemonium celebration in the Polo Grounds was led by Giants Manager, Leo Durocher. Leo managed from the field with his team at bat in the third base coaching box. (This made it much easier to relay the stolen pitching signs to the batter. The real truth was not truly known on this one momentous pitch until fifty years later, when it was finally admitted by Thomson in 2001 in a *Wall Street Journal* article by Joshua Prager. Thomson could not have known what was about to dramatically unfold, but the slugger did know exactly which pitch was coming. Its sign was transmitted from telescope to coach to bullpen to Leo in the box and to him at the plate.)

Salt-of-the-earth Leo was more salt poured on this new, deep wound—having always been a Dodger fan favorite. Durocher was not just a modern-day celebrity but an icon, on and off the field. Durocher[2] ended

---

[2] Paul Dickson's book, *Leo Durocher – Baseball's Prodigal Son*, is not only the definitive biography of Durocher's 70 years in the game.

his storied 17-year playing career not just as a Brooklyn infielder, but as their player-manager since 1939—skippering the team for nearly a decade, earning one pennant. Leo shockingly changed his allegiance, and his employment, to the Giants over a contract dispute in the middle of the 1948 season.

The Dodgers lose again, this time defeated by the most decisive dinger in baseball history—a 279-foot-long, or rather, -short, blast. I wonder in how many parks, at the time, Thomson's homer could be swatted any shorter. I had no desire to look this one up.

Finally, my cocktail tale closing: "I can honestly say that my father was not happy to see his firstborn child." Usually this begets smiles, and most of the time, laughs. In one form or another, I related that family story way too many times not to believe it. At least, not until I started researching this book.

Besides the newspaper, I am in possession of my birth certificate. Upon inspection of the two, I found that the above tale does not compute. Upon curiously reviewing the second playoff game's box score in my aged *New York Times*, I noticed the start time of today's game. It was a day game at 1:30 p.m. My birth certificate

---

It is a history book of both Major League Baseball and Americana, from Prohibition to the Astrodome. The research and writing are truthful. The story is not always pretty or rosy.

claims I was born at 2:00 *a.m.* My cocktail tale was a tall one—and dead wrong. I researched birth records of a hospital which no longer exists and baseball archives, which do, and found my lifelong understanding was erroneous. I was confused, but not perturbed. The Giants did still create infamous baseball history on the day I was born. My perception of our family's day, the sequence of its events, was somehow amiss.

I called family members. None had a memory or recollection of the facts to back my perennial cocktail story. This really made me start to wonder about myself. I consulted with my last remaining uncle, Freddie. Fred is ninety years young, ten years younger than dad, similarly born in Brooklyn and still lives in Queens. Similarly, to no avail and like almost everyone, he recalled exactly where *he* was when Bobby hit his shot, but he had no clue as to the whereabouts of his brother. (He did, however, provide an enlightening footnote*).

Unquestionably there is a locked intersection of game and birth, but did I invent the tale for ice-breaking cocktail conversation? After all, I had been in sales...I was still confused, and, frankly, stuck with my writing.

Coincidentally and fortuitously, I came across a letter from my dad which began like this:

I was asked to write this note to you, in connection with your retreat weekend. I do not find it hard to write, except how to say it!

On Oct. 3, 1951, the day you were born, you brought

joy and happiness to your mom and me. The Dodgers were beating the Giants by two runs, one out to go, (I was an avid Dodger Fan), it could not have been a more perfect day in my life. But, when I left the hospital to go home and tell the family of our joy, I heard a loud noise at the corner; Thompson hit a three-run home run; the Dodgers lost the pennant. I did not feel too bad; after all, we had a son, healthy, and all was well with our newly growing family. Your mother and I were very happy to say the least.

The game details were close enough, especially after forty years. Finding the letter was a gift for me. I suppose helping Mom and Dad feel better on that day was my gift to them.

I wonder what it was like to be there, that day. The entire game was intense. The final inning notched it up to a frenzied crescendo. To experience the game's drama today, read award-winning author Don DeLillo's short, fictional piece, *Pafko at the Wall*, a masterpiece of American sportswriting.

I was there once—in the Polo Grounds, I mean to say. 1962 was the year of the National League's return to New York and the inaugural season of my favorite team, the New York Mets. While the city constructed their first home, Shea Stadium, in Flushing, Queens, the Mets played their first two years in the unoccupied Polo Grounds. (The Giants also evacuated to the west coast in the same year as the Dodgers in 1958.)

Over my life I have been lucky enough to attend

CHAPTER 2

games in a number of baseball's cathedrals—Wrigley Field, Fenway Park, Tiger Stadium, the original Yankee Stadium, and the Polo Grounds. Never in Ebbets Field, however. The home of the Dodgers from 1913 until 1957 was demolished in 1960. The Polo Grounds followed (razed in 1964). Today, both parks have been replaced, marked by a high-rise apartment complex or a public housing project.

* Uncle Freddie knew exactly where he was when Hodges called Thomson's shot on the radio. Fred just could not believe his ears. (Not just because he was working in a loud coffee plant in Manhattan—where my dad had swung him a job just out of high school. He graduated in the year I was born). He distinctly recalled another game as well—a regular season game also between the Dodgers and Giants, to which he accompanied Mom and Dad earlier that same year. The friendly confines of Ebbets Field were not really friendly when it came to their narrow, hard, cold seats. He remembers carrying a pillow for his sister-in-law's seating comfort. She was with child (me) at the time, which gave me a revelation! I *did* attend games in each of the three baseball cathedrals of New York—the original Yankee Stadium, the Polo Grounds, and now, newly discovered (and technically speaking), EBBETS FIELD!

The Late City Edition of *The New York Times*, October 4, 1951, reported the game with two articles and a photograph. Beneath a photo of the 5'10 Durocher hugging the 6'2 Thomson, the headline reads, "It's Like a Wake in Brooklyn As Fans 'Replay' Fatal 9th."

The lead sentence in one article reads, "All Gotham was divided yesterday into three parts. The first of these the lordly Yankees inhabit; the second is the joyful country of the Giants; the third belongs to the fiercest and most desperate of all, the Brooklyn Dodgers."

I noticed at the top of the front page a small banner celebrating the newspaper's one-hundredth anniversary: 1851–1951.

In 1951, then, an October 3 trifecta: a wake, a birth, and an anniversary.

CHAPTER 3

1ST INNING - "JOLTIN JOE" & THE "KID"

July 28, 1962

It was another hot New York summer, but this particular day was gentler than most, not highly humid and in the 80s. I was on my way to being 11 years young, and also on my way to a New York Yankees game.

My dad was taking my brother, Bernard, and me to Yankee Stadium. The House that Ruth Built was not necessarily Dad's first choice, but due to circumstances beyond his control, the ballpark had become his only choice. The National League had deserted New York City in 1957. Both the Dodgers and the Giants relocated to California. (The New York Metropolitans (Mets) were born this same year, 1962, their inaugural one, via Major League Baseball NL expansion).

For five years he, and therefore we, was stuck with the Yankees as the city's only team. The Bronx Bombers always seemed to win. They would make it to the World Series and, more times than not, win there too. This was not the case for the Dodgers when they were in Brooklyn. This must have felt unfamiliar and likely uncomfortable for Dad, and for that matter, Mom.

Our seats were in the highest upper deck inside the original Yankee Stadium and were situated halfway between home plate and first base. The location also positioned us, luckily, just to the left of one of those huge blue steel posts. These steel beams had their primary purpose of holding up the stadium roof. The structures also seemed purposely and perfectly positioned to block the view of the unknowing and unlucky fan.

I realize now why Dad selected this particular game. It certainly was a way for his kids to see the great Yankees, with Mickey Mantle, Roger Maris, Whitey Ford, and Yogi Berra. It also enabled him to see the National League players whom he once watched as a kid when he lived on Montrose Avenue, and when the Dodgers still roamed Flatbush, battling their National League competition seventy-two times each season. Now his only choice was to witness them via a time machine of sorts, at an Old Timers' Day Game, on an American League diamond. It was better than nothing.

We had been living in Yonkers for nearly seven years. Dad bought our first and only family home in the same year when Brooklyn won their first and only World Series Championship in 1955, the year of the *Boys of Summer*.

CHAPTER 3

This particular Old Timers' Day was to honor and commemorate the 1937 All-Star Game. That midsummer classic occurred in Washington, DC, where I now reside. Back then, the American League team beat the National League squad in Griffith Stadium 8–3.

I distinctly remember Joe DiMaggio, the Yankee Clipper, being honored with a special commemorative watch during the pre-game introductions. Joe's career was short and spanned just thirteen seasons. World War II interrupted it. Military service gathered in three years of his playing prime at the ages of 28–30.

DiMaggio was an All Star in each season, thirteen of thirteen. He led the Yankees to the World Series in ten of those years. They were victorious in nine.

I certainly hope that watch was at least a Rolex. He more than deserved one.

DiMaggio retired in 1951, the same year Mickey Mantle made his Major League playing debut—and the year in which I was born.

The Old Timers' affair, an exhibition match before the day game, began. The Yanks were playing the Chicago White Sox, one of the teams which was a part of my first World Series memory, three years earlier in 1959.

DiMaggio, with a career .325 lifetime batting average, came to bat in the first inning. An American League Old Timer was already on board, standing on first base. Joe D was facing former Brooklyn Dodger righthander,

Van Lingle Mungo, who led the NL in ERA (2.87) that year and has to possess one of the best baseball names ever.

Hall of Fame catcher Ernie Lombardi, a Cincinnati Red and that year's NL MVP, gave the sign to Mungo. On a full count (two strike, three ball pitch) Joltin' Joe connected, hitting one squarely, sending it well over four hundred feet to deep center field. Jo-Jo Moore, a 12-year, career-long New York Giant left fielder, today playing out of position, gave chase. DiMaggio was coasting into second base when Moore tripped trying to catch the drive. The crowd began screaming for DiMaggio to keep running, which he obliged, despite his huffing and puffing. Joe reached third when the centerfielder finally caught up with his ball, and now the crowd was yelling even louder. Moore relayed it into the shortstop, Dick Bartell, another former New York Giant, who fired a strike to home plate, which Joe barely beat for an inside-the-park home run.

What a treat, to say the least! And we had not even begun to watch Maris, Mantle, Berra, and Ford yet!

The *Chairman of the Board* was the starting pitcher in the day's official affair. Whitey Ford grew up in Astoria, Queens and played baseball beneath the 59th Street Bridge (Queensborough Bridge). Ford was raised in the same neighborhood that produced Sam Mele and Anthony Benedetto. The former was a Major League player and Minnesota Twin World Series Manager; the lat-

CHAPTER 3

ter did not play professional baseball but left his heart in San Francisco.

Local Yankee scouts noticed Whitey's potential. In a summer league in 1946, with Ford as its key starting pitcher, the 34th Avenue Boys marked a record of 36–0, which was fairly consistent.

Twelve years later, I and the mother of my children would be residing at three different addresses in the neighborhood next to Whitey's, in Jackson Heights. One location would be our first, but definitely not last, house.

A future Hall of Fame pitcher himself, Ford was the previous year's Cy Young Award Winner, accruing 25 wins. On this particular afternoon, Whitey was not the vintage Whitey. Ford was yanked in the fifth inning. The White Sox were up 3–0.

After the stretch in the seventh inning, Yankee #7, Mickey Mantle, took his turn to bat. The Mick promptly hit a rocket, depositing it into the upper-right field deck and moving the score to 3–1.

The Bombers put two more runners on the basepaths. Perennial Yankee Manager, Casey Stengal, then inserted a pinch hitter into the lineup—his trusty pinch-hitter-catcher-outfielder, Johnny Blanchard. Blanchard delivered and sent another deep home run into the right field stands, plating three runs and establishing a Yankee 4–3 lead. This score painstakingly and eventually became the final one.

To accomplish this, Stengal needed to make another switch—this time on the pitching side, in the final inning. Rookie Jim Bouton saved the game with just one (maybe) pitch, rescuing the struggling closer, Luis Arroyo, who had led the league in Saves in the previous year. The final White Sox lined into a game-ending double play.

In the next season Bouton, in 249 innings, would go on to win 21 games and register a 2.53 ERA in his only All-Star season. That one season accounted for 33 percent of the victories of his 10-year career. He also pitched one game in the World Series which he lost, but respectably 1–0, to Hall of Fame pitcher Don Drysdale of the Los Angeles Dodgers. In the following year, 1964, he won both World Series games he started against the St. Louis Cardinals, but the Yanks could not solve Hall of Famer pitcher Bob Gibson.

Eight years later, Bouton authored *Ball Four,* based on a diary of his season with the Seattle Pilots, an expansion team with a life of just one year. The Pilots became the Milwaukee Brewers when Bud Selig purchased them. Selig was destined to be the Commissioner of Major League Baseball, and its Steward of Steroids.

Ball Four was popular. It was also very unpopular, with Major League Baseball and its dependent sports media. This was unsurprising, since the one-year memoir exposed the truth. I recall reading it in paperback form in my freshman year at college. I absolutely loved it. I might have read it three times. I recall leaving pages tattered. Readers absorbed details and savored its stories. It was about baseball and the real world of the players, inside and outside the lines, before and after the game.

Since the Pilots finished 45 games out of first place in their inaugural and only season, I am conjecturing that Bouton welcomed the diversion of a book or diary, or probably anything, while sitting out in the bullpen. I can totally relate to this possibility as I attempt to author whatever this writing becomes during a pandemic.

Summary:

1951: Joe DiMaggio retired.
1951: Mickey Mantle debuted.
1951: I was born.
1951: Thomson hits the *Shot Heard Round the World*
1962: Retired DiMaggio hits an inside-the-park home run in Yankee Stadium.
1962: Mantle hits an upper-deck home run—on the same day, in the same place.

Coincidence?

No. 5
Mickey Mantle
NEW YORK YANKEES — OUTFIELDER
Ht.—6'; Wt.—200; Switch Hitter; Throws—Right; Born—October 20, 1931; Home—Dallas, Texas

The AL's home-run king for the 4th time in 1960 (40), he also finished 2nd for the MVP Award. Mickey won the MVP title in 1956, with a BA of .353, and again in 1957 with a BA of .365 (his all-time high). He has hit 14 World Series HR's—one behind Ruth's record of 15. He ranks 6th in lifetime HR's with 374. All-Star Games (1953-1961).

MAJOR LEAGUE BATTING RECORD

	Games	At Bat	Runs	Hits	2B	3B	HR	RBI	Avg.
1961	153	514	131	163	16	6	54	128	.317
LIFE	1,552	5,519	1,244	1,700	241	66	374	1,063	.308

No. 7
Yogi Berra
NEW YORK YANKEES — OUTFIELDER — CATCHER
Ht.—5'8"; Wt.—191; Bats—Left; Throws—Right; Born—May 12, 1925; Home—Montclair, New Jersey

Yogi has just about re-written the record books—both as a batter and receiver. In World Series play (including 1961) he has played in the most series (12), has the most hits (71), most total bases (117), and RBI's (39). He cracked out his 2000th hit on June 28, 1961. He holds the record for most HR's as a catcher (298).

MAJOR LEAGUE BATTING RECORD

	Games	At Bat	Runs	Hits	2B	3B	HR	RBI	Avg.
1961	119	395	62	107	12	0	22	61	.271
LIFE	1,966	7,167	1,129	2,053	308	49	340	1,367	.286

CHAPTER 4

2ND INNING - BRONX BEDLAM

October 14, 1976

I was lucky enough to attend and, much more importantly, graduate from a great high school which is situated on the Grand Concourse in the south Bronx of New York City. Opened in 1941 and constructed in the art deco style, the building is located just blocks away from a number of bustling, standout landmarks, including the Bronx Supreme Court House; the full city block-sized U.S. Post Office between 149th and 150th Streets; the Bronx House of Detention at River Avenue; and the diverse Cash & Carry Bronx Terminal Market located on the interior of Exterior Street, tucked away beneath the Major Deegan Expressway (with its aliases of New York State Thruway and Interstate 87).

The last three landmarks are no longer, and while the former two are still bustling, they have been demolished and resurrected as a destination shopping center.

In the 60s and 70s, the Court House was a regularly noticed, boxlike structure on televised New York Yankee ballgames on Channel 11 (WPIX). It served as an official, municipal backdrop located in full view beyond the 461' marker on the center field wall, adorned nearby by Ballantine and Schaefer Beer ads.

I recall viewing it often. This was no small task—to do so meant you must be able to follow the upward trajectory of a Yogi Berra- or Mickey Mantle-launched home run shot. Occasionally there was the additional distraction of the rumbling, elevated #4 Train, also in full view, on Jerome Avenue, rattling its northward way to Woodlawn. The battered balls would either nestle gently into the glove of a loyal bleacher fan or rattle around aimlessly, for minutes it seemed, among rows of lonely, empty seats—unless game attendance was over 40,000 - which would, in itself, be yet another distraction.

Cardinal Hayes High School is an all-boys, New York City diocesan educational institution, one of the few Catholic schools still standing, left to its own, over 80 years later. Highly regarded, Hayes has a reputation for quality teaching and a tradition of instilling discipline into its student body, transforming boys into men in four quick years. The Athletics Department usually produces competitive teams and is a member of one of the nation's premiere high school sports leagues, the New York Metro CHSAA (Catholic High School Athletic Association), which has graduated the likes of NBA stars Kareem Abdul-Jabbar (Lew Alcindor), Jamal Mashburn, Chris Mullins, Kenny Smith, and many, many others, as well as players and coaches in the National Football League—most notably, Vince Lombardi—and MLB greats, like John Candelaria and Joe Torre.

As the crow, or Cardinal, flies, the school's front doors are no further than fifteen hundred feet from the House that Ruth built. Back then, the school's site for outdoor fall and spring physical education (gym class), in both good and sometimes harsh weather, was a short stroll (or quick dash in short gym shorts) down to Macombs Dam Park. The facility was an open, cavernous complex, complete with full track and field facilities, located in the shadow of Yankee Stadium.

I had done academically and behaviorally well enough to earn a partial scholarship to Manhattan College, another all-male, New York City, Catholic learning institution, not located in Manhattan. I decided to take the money and run to Riverdale, also located in the Bronx, but definitely not south.

Founded in 1853 by the Brothers of the Christian Schools, a teaching order started by Saint John Baptist de La Salle—patron saint of teachers—had the school color of Kelly Green and a school nickname of: the Jaspers. A Jasper? A wolf in the wild, a mountain lion, a mineral of red quartz (wrong color, if we were green)...a puzzlement? Truth is that the Jasper we were named after was human.

Brother Jasper Brennan was a part of the faculty in the nineteenth century. He taught history, and doubled as the school's first Athletic Director. Brother Jasper brought the little-known sport of baseball to campus in the early 1880s. In addition to coaching the college's inaugural teams, literally instructing the students on how to play the new game, he was also responsible for the conduct of student fans, who were not allowed to move from their seats until the game was over. He tripled as the college's Prefect of Discipline.

Annually, the college team played semi-pro squads. One was the Metropolitans (not yet the New York Mets). The site usually was the Polo Grounds, a stadium located on Coogan's Hollow Blough at 155th Street, overlooking the Harlem River, directly across from the site later to be Yankee Stadium, which would eventually be 1500 feet from the front doors of the still later-to-be Cardinal Hayes High School.

As the story goes, Brother Jasper would notice that on one especially hot June day in 1882, at a Metropolitan game, the fans would be stirring and getting restless, even more so in the latter innings and hours in the sun. His student conduct policy of sitting in one's place for the entire game seemed untenable. Brother Jasper called a timeout before the bottom of the seventh inning and allowed the students to get up and stretch for a few minutes. This became a standard at every home game.

When the New York Giants saw it for themselves during an exhibition game between the two teams, they liked the tradition so much that they brought it into their games in the Polo Grounds. The school's practice of the "seventh inning stretch" spread into the major leagues, and is now a baseball tradition forever.

My first year in college was spectacular, and not just because it was the first year of legal drinking eligibility. In 1969 the New York Football Jets, the New York NBA Knicks, and the Miracle New York Mets, all three, won World Championships. Their exciting seasons and successful playoff runs were thankful diversions from the stressors of the world we lived in at the time—not the least of which was the Vietnam War.

In addition to off-campus adult education, I majored in Business Administration, specifically Marketing. I progressed through four years of curriculum, earning a college diploma handed to me in Madison Square Garden on the stage of its once Felt Forum.

General Foods Corporation, destined to become a part of Kraft Foods, had already hired me on campus. Job interviews occurred at the Career Planning Center, which was located in a rickety, wooden, white structure named Azarius Hall. The building once served as army barracks during World War II. Today, it also no longer exists, as a part of Draddy Gymnasium sits atop it.

I signed up to be a rookie recruit in an elite army: Maxwell House Division's salesforce. My first sales territory was a "trip list" of supermarkets located in the familiar south Bronx. Within two years, MHD promoted me to Account Manager. This job required travel from Queens, where I had settled, to the distant state of New Jersey. My company car and I traveled through Brooklyn, across Staten Island, usually over the Verrazano Narrows Bridge, to the corporate headquarters offices of two once powerful, but now also nonexistent supermarket companies: Pathmark and Foodtown.

By this point, I had already met and married my wife, Maria. While at college we had run into each other on one of those nights at one of those bars at one of those campus foothills in Riverdale. I am eternally grateful that, for at least that one night, I was clear-eyed enough to recognize beauty in front of me.

Maria's dad was a well-known television and radio broadcaster in New York's Spanish media marketplace. Eusebio Valls eventually rose to become the news anchor of a television station and an emerging network, Telemundo. He anchored the nightly television news broadcast, Monday through Friday, on channel 47, WNJU (call letters: Newark, New Jersey). I thought it was pretty cool to be able to flip the channel and watch my father-in-law on TV, Monday through Friday at 10:30

p.m., soon after sharing dinner or a beer with him in Jackson Heights (Queens).

Valls had had a high-profile television and media career in Havana, Cuba. In the early 60s, shortly after personally interviewing Fidel Castro, he decided to exit his native land with his wife and young daughter.

In New York, Valls was also the Yankee game announcer for the Spanish radio station WHOM in the mid-60s. Unfortunately, this was just for a short while. More unfortunately it was at a time when the Bronx Bombers had temporarily lost their way, with a newly found habit of not winning.

He personally knew many Major League ballplayers and their families because of winter ball on the island, such as Bob Allison, Chuck Connors (see the TV series: *The Rifleman*), and others.

He knew many Cuban ball players as well, many already playing in the Majors. The Cuban Comet, Minnie Minosa, is a stellar example. Minnie was the first Black Hispanic in the Major Leagues (1949), the first Black player of the Chicago White Sox, a nine-time All Star, and, finally now, in the Hall of Fame.

Admittedly, this may seem a lengthy preamble for the description of this *chronicle* and *connection*. That is the point, after all, and the point of this book; my connections and their multiple threads support the basis of my theory.

In this case, if I had not attended Cardinal Hayes (vs. the usually attended Yonkers high school) I probably would not have attended Manhattan College. I would probably not have met my wife, or later her father (and mother). Therefore, in this American Bicentennial year, I would not have been present in the offices of radio station WADO, located at 205 East 42nd Street, on October 14, 1976.

The sales and marketing executives of General Foods, its Maxwell House Division in particular, were beginning to understand that there were large consumer segments across the country which conversed in Spanish, watched Spanish-speaking television and programming, listened to Spanish radio, and shopped in culturally oriented retail establishments. This was not exclusive to New York City, but its metropolitan area was huge and, conveniently, nearby. Our District Manager asked me to organize a market review, a fact-finding trip for the GF executives who inhabited offices in the north, in the suburb of White Plains.

Assisted by radio connections of Valls, we arranged for a black stretch limo and a stretching urban itinerary. We conspicuously toured a dozen small and large neighborhood food stores in the south Bronx, Harlem and Elizabeth, New Jersey.

The conclusion of this group learning excursion ended in the Manhattan office of WADO's President. After a standing, impromptu, 10-minute meeting, our host announced that he had a scheduling problem that same evening. He was in the fortunate possession of

CHAPTER 4

two pairs of tickets to two conflicting, but important sporting events. One was a regular season NHL hockey game—New York Islanders vs. the New York Rangers, blocks away at Madison Square Garden. It was a hot ticket and one which he personally had no choice but to punch. Unfortunately for him, the others were for two box seats to the fifth and final game of the American League Championship Series between the New York Yankees and the Kansas City Royals. He offered these tickets to us.

I looked at my boss, who looked at his boss—both stated they couldn't attend. I snatched them up and immediately sought out the nearest public payphone. There was a wide selection curbside, at that time.

I called Valls in Queens. I suggested that he should call in sick tonight. We were going to the game. He answered *"How can I do that? I would not be able to make it to the Manhattan studio in time for the News."*

I responded simply: *"Valls, you have no choice, this is baseball. This is the Yankees in Yankee Stadium, a Final Game Five. They have stunk for more than a decade and have not been to their usual World Series since 1964. This is their chance."*

Suddenly feeling ill, Valls called in sick.

The seats were great. Field box level on the first base side, an excellent value (since they were free). Their stubs showed an official face value of $8.00.

The game, like the series, was a seesaw affair. The Royals scored first in the first via John Mayberry's two-run home run. The Yanks immediately tied it up in the same inning 2-2. KC promptly took a one run lead in the next inning. The Bombers then built their new lead up to 6-3, plating two in the third and two more in the in the sixth. They carried this advantage into the next-to-last inning. The 58,000 plus stadium spectators were raucous and ready.

In the top of the eighth inning, the Royals batted two singles against two Yankee pitchers. A home run followed, knotting the game again, now 6-6. This came courtesy of Hall of Fame third baseman, George Brett. This Royal was a terror at the plate and came the closest to hitting .400 since Ted Williams. You talk about putting water on a fire—yikes! Brett's blast quickly quieted the stunned crowd. Young relief pitcher Mark Littell mowed down the Yankees, 1-2-3, in their half of the inning.

In the top of the ninth inning, the Yankees escaped a two on, two out jam and held Kansas City off the board. There was a delay to the bottom of the ninth—fans were throwing trash onto the field, evidently cranking up for their team's last at-bat, (or just tidying up around their seats). Littell had already warmed up, but now was just standing around during the garbage cleanup. It was getting very chilly, now dipping down into the 30s. This might end up being a long season ending, an extra inning game. I was not in possession of the proper attire.

The Yankee leadoff batter was clean-up hitter, Chris Chambliss. He had come over from the Cleveland Indians in the previous year and had been Rookie of the Year in 1971. My scorecard showed that he already had a productive night, with a double and driving in two runs. He was also red hot, hitting over .500 and now with seven runs batted in for the series.

Then, as quick as that, Chambliss hit the first pitch thrown and bombed a season-winning walk-off home run. The Stadium shook, the fans went crazy (or crazier), pouring out onto the field...Yankees victorious, 7–6! Heading to the World Series!

In the hysteria which ensued, Chambliss never was able to touch home plate. No Yankees fan would ever admit that. He was lucky enough to escape to the clubhouse with his life, let alone with his batting helmet, which he carried tucked under his arm like a fullback as he ran away from the celebrating Bronx mob.

It was one of the biggest hits in baseball history. The last one was Pittsburgh Pirate Bill Mazeroski's walk-off homer that beat these same Yankees in 1960, in Game #7 of the World Series. Under the fiery leadership of Billy Martin and the turbulent ownership of George Steinbrenner, the Bombers were back—and now, with new heroes.

There was a post-game controversy about not touching home plate. Chambliss never made it that far. The plate probably was no longer there anyway. There is no way that he came within close proximity to the plate. The other three bases had been captured and were missing. Again, he was running for his life! Manager Whitey Herzog and the Royals never truly challenged this, which is curious, since baseball is a game chock full of rules—and touching home plate to score is a pretty big one.

Baseball did add a new rule which allows umpires to award a base "because of obstruction by the fans," often referred to as the "Chris Chambliss Rule."

The next day's front page of The *Daily News* captioned a photograph of the sweet home run swing with, *"THE Shot Heard 'Round the Bronx.'"*

This was the team's 30th league pennant. Notably, it was the start of the club's resurgence, with a new cast of characters: Billy the Kid (Martin), Catfish (Hunter), Thurman (Munson), Sparky (Lyle), Mr. October (Reggie Jackson), et al.

Boy did I "luck out" with my bumping into those two free tickets earlier in the same day. I thought that I would never again be at a game as good as this.

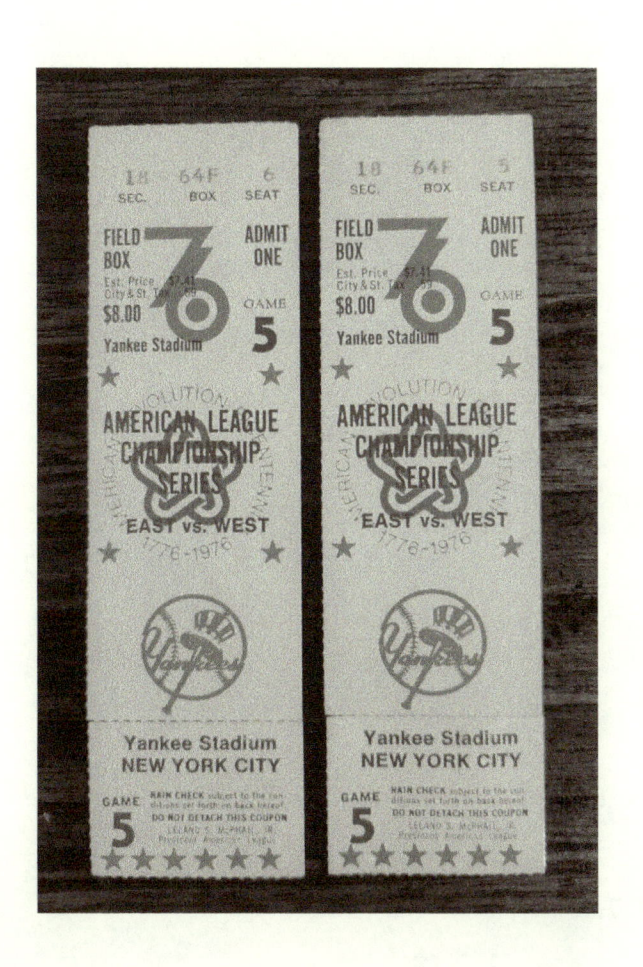

CHAPTER 4

CHAPTER 5

3RD INNING - A FUNERAL AND A ROSE

July 25, 1978

Our family's first corporate transfer with the General Foods Corporation occurred in the winter of 1977. We came down from the hills and into the valley, relocating from Jackson Heights in Queens to the Chicago suburb of Rolling Meadows. This was to be the birthplace of our first daughter, in June, who entered this world not remotely close to the meadows but rather upon the shores of Lake Michigan, which was no longer frozen.

Our long and unnerving drive to East Huron Street downtown became the classic "hurry up and wait." What followed was a 19-hour labor at Northwestern University's Prentice Women's Hospital, a newly designed, iconic structure. Developers later—controversially and ceremoniously—razed the complex, an activity which

I suddenly ran into while on an early morning downtown jog, 40 years later.

We were fortunate to have a great sales team, one with a blend of experience and youth. One tenured colleague was Big John P., who resided in nearby Palatine. His daughter was a nursing student who graciously agreed to become the first babysitter of proud new parents.

Our stay in Chicago was a frigid blur punctuated by a host of unsettling events. Examples: the death of the city's longtime mayor, John J. Daley (an overwhelming supporter of President John F. Kennedy at the 1960 Democratic Convention, as well as the city's mayor during the infamous 1968 Democratic Convention in the Windy City); the launch of Alex Haley's miniseries, *Roots*; a brutal blizzard; and a winter season marked by 43 days below freezing temperature and 82.3 inches of snow.

Then there was the business market upheaval.

Turned out, it was also cold in South America—Brazil's largest coffee-producing region was devastated by frost damage. Coffee is the second-largest traded commodity in the world, and Brazil produces one third of the world's global supply. We were suddenly selling *liquid gold*. With costs skyrocketing daily, life seemed to be all about monthly price increases, low stock levels, and controlled product allocations. It was testy times at the desks of usually testing buyers.

CHAPTER 5

The Chicago haze cleared before we knew it, and GF promoted us again—and sent us packing back to New York in the summer of 1978.

Shortly before this, Big John P. had developed stomach cancer. John was a strapping, large man of Polish descent, a south-sided White Sox fan, and father to seven. I vividly recall visiting him in the hospital—vivid, because of his rapidly reduced physical presence. I recall us talking about baseball and coffee, but definitely not about his prognosis.

Less than a month later, we heard of John's passing. Another John, Biltgen, had also been a previous teammate of John P. This John labored just two corporate cubicles away in the White Plains, NY headquarters. We quickly decided to return to Chicago for funeral services.

We arrived late Monday afternoon. Little coffee was consumed that evening, but java did become very necessary the next morning, prior to our attendance of the sad service and following lunch with John's wife, Angie, as well as their large family and friends.

As we were flying back into LaGuardia Airport, being the summer and baseball season, I noticed in the newspaper that the Cincinnati Reds were in town and scheduled to play my favorite team, the increasingly uncompetitive New York Mets. More importantly, Pete Rose was on the front and back page, in addition to being in the sports section of every New York City tabloid.

This night was going to be his night: a chance to break the National League's consecutive-game hitting streak of 37 games (the record was set in 1945 by the then-Boston Brave Tommy Holmes).

After hitting in the 36th consecutive game, Rose was quoted saying he really did not feel any pressure and that there was no reason he could not hit in another one.

I looked over to John Biltgen and said, "Hey, you want to go to the Mets game tonight?"

Eyeing the headlines, this other John said, "Hell yes! We could use something else to think about."

After purchasing our tickets at Shea Stadium's box office ticket window minutes before the first pitch, we hurried to our nosebleed seats in the upper deck above left field. Rose batted leadoff. Charlie Hustle did not disappoint. In his second at-bat, he hit a single off right-handed pitcher Craig Swan in front of a crowd of over 38,000, made up of mostly New Yorkers. Rose finished going three for four. Mets fans that night wore T-shirts reading, "I saw Pete Rose do it." I decided not to purchase one. It was baseball, not The Beatles or the Pope. In his last year managing the aging Big Red Machine, Cincinnati Manager Sparky Anderson commented after the game in wonderment, "They were getting $4.50 for those shirts and selling Mets banners for a buck and a half."

CHAPTER 5

Shortly after witnessing the record-breaking hit, I looked over to my fellow eyewitness and asked if he wanted to depart—we had seen what we had come for. Comfortably beating the usual crowd, we walked out of the stadium and headed to the nearby airport parking garage. We then commenced our separate, solemn drives home.

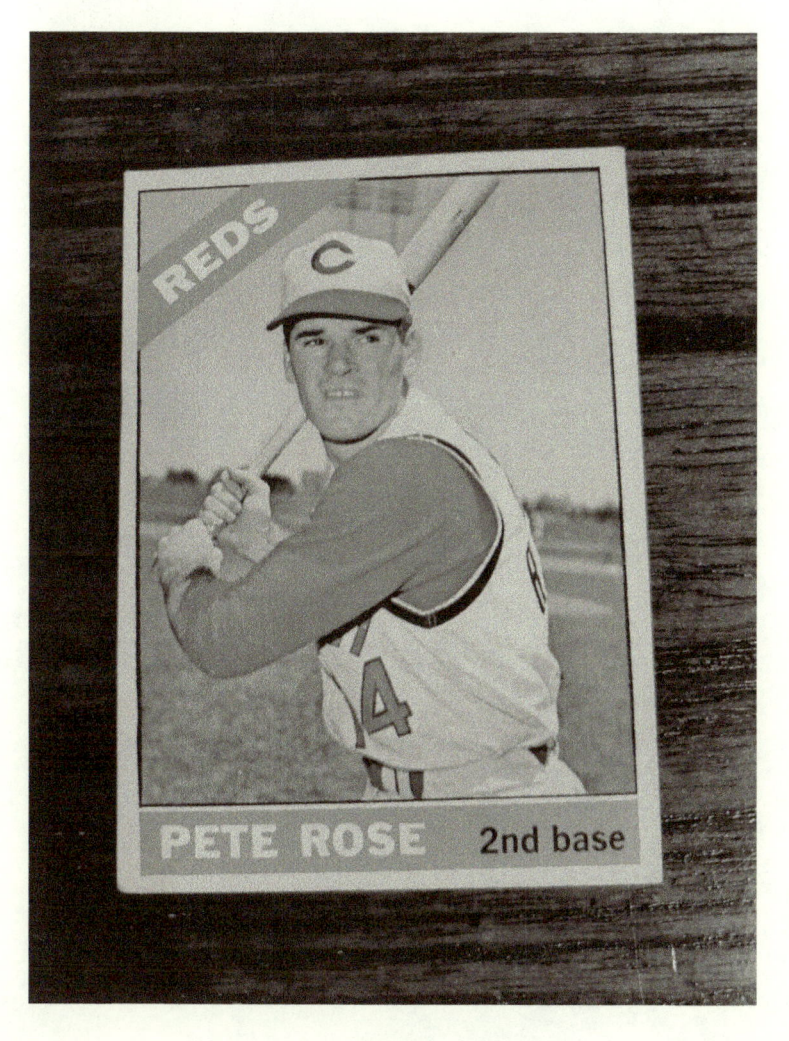

CHAPTER 6

4TH INNING - ROYAL PAIN

October 19, 1980

The family was transferred once again, turned around from New York to the Midwest, but this time to Kansas City.

It was March, so no baseball yet, but it was still an enjoyable time for any fan anywhere. With hot stove season behind us, the baseball enthusiast was glued to newspaper coverage and the meaningless spring training box scores of their favorite team. Hope springs eternal.

Timing is everything, and this time it was particularly good. I was young for this level of job—District Manager, not yet 30 years of age. My sales domain encompassed the four states of Missouri, Kansas, Oklahoma, and Arkansas. This was another quick stop, but we did manage to take in the sights—such as the Harry

Truman Museum in Independence, a birds-eye view of a small Kansas tornado cutting its path across an open farm field, the Cowboy Hall of Fame, and Hot Springs National Park in the Ouachita Mountains.

Maxwell House owned season tickets to the Kansas City Royals. As an expansion team, it was also young—12 years young, to be exact. The Royals were born in 1969, which also was the first year in which an expansion team had reached the World Series (that particular club hailed from Queens).

In New York, our family had survived the experience of its first home ownership, complete with quite an educational experience of land-lordship. We escaped both the city's, and baseball's, Bronx Burning, leaving behind Billy the Kid, Mr. October, and Shipbuilder Steinbrenner. The Yankees had achieved two consecutive, exciting World Series Championships, conquering both times the Dodgers, which now resided in Los Angeles.

For three consecutive years, these same Yankees vanquished these same Royals—starting in a year which you should remember (see the *2nd Inning chapter*).

That was in the 70s. This was a new decade. Things were destined to be distinctly different. The Royals were still incredibly good, but they were getting even better, each and every day. Even the casual fan could notice. With season tickets, I luckily(?) was able to entertain customers along with members of the sales team while attending as many games as possible.

Opening Day, April 10, took place at night, in the dark—an opening day first, at least for me. Dennis Leonard, who was born in Brooklyn (also in 1951), was the Royals' starting pitcher. Leonard was drafted from Iona College in New Rochelle, New York. Just four years earlier, I had earned an MBA, my graduate degree, on the same campus. The righty was the ace of the Royal staff and a genuine workhorse. Two years earlier, he had hurled 21 complete games and amassed 244 strikeouts in over 294 innings. He also led the league in games started (40) and batters faced (1,218).

On this day—or rather, night—Dennis lost to the Tigers and to Hall of Famer Jack Morris 5–1. The Royals then won the next three games to take the series from Detroit. In his next outing in Baltimore, Leonard lost again—and this time to another Hall of Famer, Jim Palmer. From there, he went on to win 20 games and became the only pitcher in Royals history to achieve three 20-game winning seasons.

But that was just for openers. Fans were treated to a fabulously Royal ride all season long:

- George Brett hit .390, almost catching up to the improbable barrier of .400 (Ted Williams achieved that last, with a .406 in 1941); he was named the American League's MVP.

- Willie Wilson almost caught up to 100 stolen bases, swiping 79.
- Relief pitcher Dan Quisenberry did catch up with the Yankee Goose, Gossage (see the *5th Inning chapter*) with 33 saves, in addition to 12 wins.
- And much more

Said another way, 1980 was Baseball Rock 'n' Roll in Missouri (and Kansas). Their 97 wins that season still stand as the most in franchise history.

Undoubtedly, this royal steamroller was poised to win the Western Division. The only question remaining was which team they would have to beat in the league championship series to claim their first ticket to the Fall Classic.

Well, of course, it would be the Yankees. Again. This time, they were coming in with only 103 wins. This would be their fourth consecutive confrontation. The manager of the Royals was Jim Frey, for this, his one and only year. The Yankee skipper was Dick Howser, who, in short order, would also relocate to here, becoming the KC manager in the following year. (Howser began his playing career with the Kansas City Athletics and ended it with the New York Yankees. It's all right if you are feeling whiplash.)

The Royals swept the usually formidable Bronx Bombers, winning three consecutive playoff games. The Series was punctuated with a Royal exclamation point. In the final game, contested at Yankee Stadium, George Brett whacked a come-from-behind, three-run home run off of Goose Gossage (see the *5th Inning chapter,* again) in the seventh inning, crushing the Yanks along with the hopes of the Yankee faithful.

The young Royals then moved on to their first World Series to face the Philadelphia Phillies. The Phils were led by their own MVP third baseman, Mike Schmidt.

I attended regular season games with my sales teammate, Greg Price. We would observe more than the regular intricacies of the game. Greg had played college baseball at the University of Central Arkansas not that long before. Like me, Greg was also lucky to be young for his job.

There we both sat for another ballgame, but this one was the pivotal World Series Game #5. The Phillies had won the first two games in Philadelphia. The Royals responded, winning the next two games here in Missouri. The whole town was now in the midst of a 48-hour, baseball championship fog—and hangover.

Two nights prior, Willie Mays Aikens finished a tip and tuck, tied game with a walk-off RBI single in the 10th inning. He followed that with an encore performance in Game #4, cracking two home runs with three RBIs in a 5–3 victory.

Unlike these last two games, today was not a night game and was played in the sun and the shadows of late afternoon. The Royals held a 3–2 lead going into the last inning. Submarine style pitcher and American League save leader, Dan Quisenberry, was still on the mound. He had entered the game earlier than normal, as he seemed to have been doing often in the World Series.

Just three more outs—all felt well- for a minute.

Before you could swallow your first sip of your planned celebratory frosty, the Royals were losing 4–3. The Philadelphia method was not pretty. They had passed the batting baton effectively. Schmidt led off with an infield base hit just off Brett's glove at third base, followed by a bouncing double down the first base line, a bunt, and a groundout—that meant two runs penciled reluctantly into your scorecard.

In their last at-bat, the Royals loaded the bases with two outs, creating a near thrilling end to the game. The Philly reliever pitcher was none other than Tug McGraw. Tug was a member of the 1969 New York Mets, which were the first expansion team to win a World Series.

As quickly as Tug created this final inning jam, he fanned Jose Cardenal for the final out to end it. The Phil closer closed out the last three innings with five strikeouts and sent the two teams off to the city of Brotherly Love. That site turned out not to be very brotherly to the Royals—they lost the next game and their first World Series. The Phillies had won their first ever, which had taken them nearly 100 years. The club's origin was in 1883 (as the Philadelphia Quakers).

Notable factoids of this WS:

- Tug McGraw figured in four of the six games: 1 W, 1 L, 2 Saves.
- Dan Quisenberry figured in four of the six games: 1 W, 2L, 1 Save.
- Mike Schmidt was the MVP with 2 HRs 7 RBIs and hit .381.
- Willie Aikens recorded 4 HRs, 8 RBIs and batted .400—and was not the MVP.
- Royal center fielder Amos Otis had 3 HRs, 7 RBIs, hit .478, and also was not the MVP.
- Royal leadoff hitter, Willie Wilson, had 26 plate appearances and struck out in 12 of them, a World Series record. He did manage to steal two bases.
- Hall of Fame players included Brett, Schmidt, and Steve Carlton (and Pete Rose).
- 1980 was the first year of ABC's television contract with MLB and their broadcast of this Series remains tied for the highest overall television ratings of all time. It was also the first Series played entirely on artificial turf.
- The NBC television broadcasting crew was Joe Garagiola, Tony Kubek, and Tom Seaver*.
- The CBS Radio broadcasters were Vince Scully and Sparky Anderson (see the 5th Inning chapter, yet again).

*While researching and writing this in August of 2020, the greatest New York Mets player ever, leader of the first expansion team to appear in and also win a World Series, Hall of Fame pitcher Tom Seaver, passed away.

I stopped writing to read Bill Madden's new book, *Tom Seaver, A Terrific Life.* I am glad that I did, not just for reading about the storied life and career of the Franchise, but for reflecting about much more than baseball.

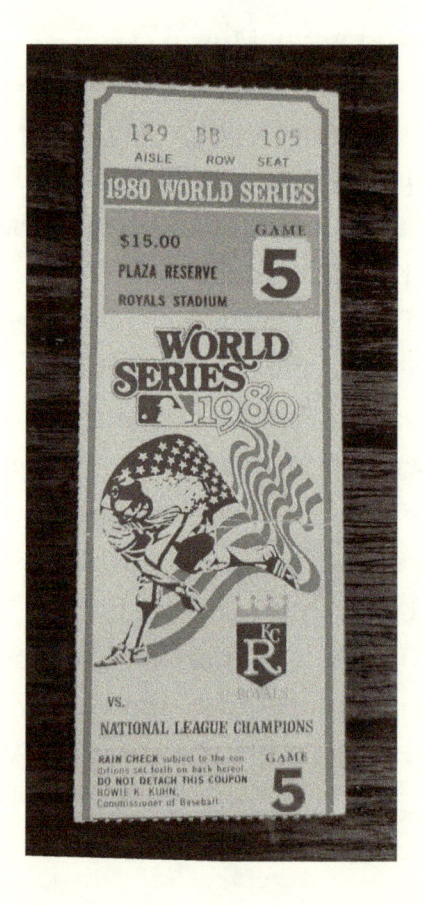

CHAPTER 7

5TH INNING - TIGER TOWN

October 14, 1984

Timing is everything, most of the time.

We relocated from Overland Park, Kansas to Farmington Hills, Michigan in 1981. The country was in the midst of its worst recession since World War II. Skyrocketing interest rates, rampant inflation, and an oil crisis forced consumer spending to go way down across the board (somewhat similar to now, post-pandemically speaking, but much worse).

Especially hard hit were large discretionary products and durable goods—such as the car.

The battered state of Detroit's auto industry was astonishing. To say it was "reeling" was neither an understatement nor a hyperbole. There was little hope for a quick recovery, or even gradual improvement. It was just plain bad.

In 1982, Michigan had achieved an unenviable #1 USA ranking: in unemployment. Its unemployment level topped 14 percent. The unemployment rate in auto assembly plant towns like Flint was higher—over 20 percent. Other areas were close behind—and not just in Michigan. The neighboring states of Indiana and Ohio were likewise heavily impacted. Towns and cities like Toledo and Lima in Ohio and Fort Wayne in Indiana joined the list of misery.

This gloomy geography encompassed our new district sales territory—not the most inspirational career opportunity. It was a generally depressing state of affairs. My new boss suggested that this new experience would be a "challenging one." Do you think? He had just terminated my predecessor.

The sales team was discouraged and in their own depressed state. At my first meeting, I looked around at the faces of my new leadership team. "Uncomforting" would be the word. Traditional platitudes like, "this too shall pass" and, "patience is a virtue" were not reasonable expectations, here. Their accounts, similar to the customers shopping in their stores, were hurting. The executives and buyers were tightening their belts. They were turning the screws.

The Detroit marketplace was also changing. The situation was fluid. Iconic, local retailers such as A&P, Kroger, and Farmer Jack were being newly challenged by new competitors. New retail giants were emerging from the western frontier. Based in Grand Rapids, Spartan and Meijer's were looking for new ways to do business. They had suggestions. We listened and negotiated.

Step by step, things slowly improved—not only in the car industry, but also with Maxwell House. The team became creative and devised innovative approaches to sales and promotion. Sales quotas were met and exceeded. Bonus checks were, thankfully, deposited in bank accounts. The company recognized the leadership team for its efforts and awarded the prestigious Chairman's Award for a successful multi-state local promotion with four municipal zoos—a big deal at the General Foods Corporation, since the Chairman presented it.

Detroit is not only a big sports town, but is a great town for sports. During our three-year stay, we experienced:

- NFL: The first winter-weather location of a Super Bowl. It was held inside the Pontiac Silverdome, and it was a good one: the thrilling Super Bowl XVI. Quarterback Joe Montana vs. Quarterback Kenny Anderson, the San Francisco 49ers vs. the Bengals of Cincinnati, the latter city less than a five-hour drive away. It was a home game for many fans…and an unfortunate outcome for their team.

- NCAA basketball: Michigan State's Magic Johnson returned to Michigan at this same Silverdome, leading his Los Angeles Lakers, along with Kareem Abdul-Jabbar, against the hometown Detroit Pistons, captained by Isiah Thomas. Attended by well over 30,000, it was the largest crowd to witness a collegiate basketball game up to that time. Many of them gained free entry with an empty can of Maxwell House coffee.
- Grand Prix: The first Formula One race held in the United States (1982). Contested on the streets of Detroit, the grueling course encircled the new Renaissance Center skyscraper complex, the tallest structure in the state. Held partly in the rain, the drivers and their engines roared through downtown streets with a view of Windsor, Canada on the Detroit River.
- NCAAF: University of Michigan football - witnessed a traditional Big Ten rivalry game of the Ohio State Buckeyes against the Michigan Wolverines. A game between these two needs to be on any serious sports fan's bucket list.
- NHL: You could be seated right behind the goalie at professional hockey games at the *new* Joe Louis Arena, welcoming the challenge of following the path of the puck while the skates of the arising Detroit Red Wings splattered chunks of ice on the plexiglass in front of you.

CHAPTER 7

However, by far, the best part of my time with sports in Detroit was baseball. Our season tickets to the Tigers were a welcomed and needed escape for us, our customers, the city, and the entire region. But to be able to enjoy a seat anywhere inside the *old* Tiger Stadium was more than an escape. It was pure joy.

Just in the prior year, Sparky Anderson (see *3rd Inning*) had similarly relocated to this Great Lakes State. His new job was Manager of the Tigers. The Yanks went on to the World Series with that dramatic Chris Chambliss walk-off home run win. It was also the last game which New York won (see *2nd Inning*). They soon ran directly into this same Sparky and the Cincinnati Reds. The Big Red Machine swept the bomber-less Bombers under the autumn rug, four games to none (4–0).

Like our sales figures, unemployment, and the auto industry, the Tigers improved each year. In 1984, team ownership changed hands—as it turned out, curiously, just for this one and only year. One of the two corporate pizza kings in town acquired the team. The owner was Irish and an alum of Notre Dame in Indiana, home to the *Fighting Irish*. So, might this be a lucky season for the Tigers?

Luck played absolutely no part in what transpired in the season of 1984 in Detroit. Serendipity may have had a hand in it.

This Tiger team was a juggernaut. Everything clicked. Hitting and pitching, batting average and home runs, starting pitching and bullpen relief. On the hitting side, they led the American League in home runs (187) and runs (829), placed second in total bases (2,436), slugging (.432) and on base percentage (.342), and placed third in batting average (.271). The pitching staff led the league in team earned run average (3.49) and games saved (51).

Spring liftoff was quick and powerful.

In their first 40 games the Tigers registered a 35–5 start. By the time the regular season's infield dust had settled, they had nearly won twice as many games as they had lost. The 104 victories are the best ever achieved in franchise history—from 1901 till today.

They led the AL's competitive East Division from start to end. They finished 15, 17, 18, or 19 games ahead of the Blue Jays, Yankees, Red Sox, and Orioles, respectively. All these teams won more games than the eventual West Division champion.

Our set of four tickets was shared among the sales team across the three states. As the season unfolded, customers with their families traveled from all directions and distances to enjoy a firsthand look at these Tigers. They were extremely popular. We were, too.

The regular season was magical. What would be the next chapter? How would it all this end when serious baseball began in October?

In the post season's first round, the Tigers faced Kansas City, winners of the West Division, an expan-

CHAPTER 7

sion team. The Royals had barely beaten out two other expansion teams, California and Minnesota, by a scant three games. The Angels and Twins had finished the campaign tied, with a .500 won-loss percentage—81 wins and 81 losses. KC ended the year with 84 wins, just six games above .500.

The Tigers had concluded their campaign a tad warmer: 58 games above .500. Most fans, and Las Vegas, expected Detroit to dominate. History does indicate that Detroit coasted through the American League Championship Series (ALCS), sweeping Kansas City (3–0). In actuality, this confrontation was much closer than its appearance in the record. The aging, but feisty opponents forced a three-game experience which was unnerving to the nervous Tiger fandom—which was eventually relieved. The Motor City was now focused on its first World Series since 1968. Territory Sales Manager Tony Aquilina and I were lucky enough to invite two executives from A&P to Game 5 of the World Series.

The San Diego Padres had bested Chicago in a five-game series, 3–2, in the National League Championship Series (NLCS). Customarily the Cubbies met their historical expectation. They had blown a two-game lead in a five-game series, losing the final three games.

The MVP of each championship series, Tiger Kirk Gibson and Padre Steve Garvey, were alumni of Michigan State University. This put an extra cherry on top for many a Michigander.

Before meeting up with our customers at the game, Tony and I dined at Armando's, our season-long pre-game ritual meal. Planning to beat the game traffic, we arrived early. More importantly, we were very aware that the baseball gods did not permit us to modify our usually successful routine.

Established in 1969, located on Vernor Highway, Armando's served the best food in Mexicantown. Dine there just once, and one will forever remember its red plastic napery as much as its food (and great margaritas). The establishment was awash in team memorabilia—autographed photographs greeted you upon entrance. It was well known that the Tigers were frequent post-game patrons; Armando's was just a five-minute drive from Tiger Stadium.

The Tigers had returned home from San Diego with the series tied, one to one. They quickly assumed their home court advantage by winning the next two games. Hall of Fame pitcher, Jack Morris, was responsible for winning two of the three victories, both accomplished by baseball's now lost, once traditional, complete game performance.

On this damp, foggy evening, 51,901 assembled at the "*Corner.*" Opening in 1912, originally named Navin Field and subsequently renamed Briggs Stadium, Tiger Stadium was tied with Fenway Park as being major league baseball's oldest diamond. Anticipation was highly hopeful that tonight's game would be the final

CHAPTER 7

one of the season, played here where Michigan met Trumbull (avenues). As San Diego's weather is the best in the country, with the exclusion of the Padres and their fans, no one was inclined to travel back there again this week to enjoy it.

Equipped with rain gear, towel, and umbrella, we settled uncomfortably into our wet, blue wooden seats. I proceeded to fill in the obligatory scorecard. My pencil was quite revealing. I had not deeply appreciated the makeup of the opponent's roster. Arguably, it was more impressive than the Tigers—maybe not in this year, but from an historical perspective. The San Diego lineup was a patchwork of not only present, but past and future World Series players, perennial and occasional All- Stars, and eventual Hall of Famers: among others, it included Manager Dick Williams, Steve Garvey, Craig Nettles, Kevin McReynolds, Tony Gwynn, Bruce Bochy, Gary Templeton, and Rich (Goose) Gossage. I appreciated more now why the friars were still standing after 171 games.

The opening inning opened swimmingly with Detroit quickly jumping out to a three-run lead, anchored by Kirk Gibson's deep two run home run shot to right centerfield, slamming the first pitched baseball that met his eyes.

The Padres scratched themselves back into the game, plating one run in the second and a pair in the fourth, knotting the score 3–3. The battle continued.

The Tigers roared right back in the next inning. Gibson was again involved in another run—this time scoring in daring fashion, tagging up on a short sacrifice fly gloved by the second baseman. His element of surprise put the Tigers up 4–3.

In this era, relief pitchers would labor for the final six or nine outs to preserve the win. It was getting close to closer time. Both teams had excellent bullpens. The go-to throwers were All Stars and baseball's cream of the crop. San Diego would tap the great Goose Gossage and Detroit would eventually call upon Willie Hernandez. The former is a Hall of Famer, one of the very few elected who specialized out of the bullpen. The latter won the American League's Cy Young Award *and* the Most Valuable Player (MVP) award in this same year.

The teams traded zeroes in the sixth, and then the Padres were scoreless in the top of the seventh. After the home crowd's stretch, and Gibson leading off by fanning, the Padres brought in their Goose. He was to face Tiger All Star catcher, Lance Parrish. Parrish promptly greeted him with a deep home run to left field, padding the late game lead for the home team, now up 5–3.

The contest's pendulum continued. Enter ace reliever Hernandez, in the top of the eighth. After getting the first two batters out on four pitches, Kurt Bevacqua hit his fifth one out for a home run. Bevacqua had hit his second World Series dinger. Incredulously, this doubled his regular season home run count, a grand to-

CHAPTER 7

tal of one, accomplished in 80 turns at bat. Tigers were still up, but now by the closer score of 5–4.

With the intimidating Goose still on the mound in the bottom of the inning, the Tigers managed to get runners to second and third base with just one out. First base was clearly open. Gibson was due up. Lance Parrish was on deck.

Pick your poison.

Padres Manager, Williams, visited the pitching mound for a meeting with Gossage. Williams wanted to walk left-hand hitting Gibson to load the bases and set up righty against righty. (Parrish had already greeted the Goose with a home run). Gossage disagreed. He convinced Williams into letting him pitch to Gibson (who had also already homered earlier in the game).

Both were wrong.

With the Tigers up by only one run, and the Padres only one game away from extinction, they decided to pitch to Kirk. Gossage was a righty, but this time he was not going to be right. Gibson launched a gigantic three-run home run into the right field upper deck. The ball nearly cleared the stadium roof, almost landing on Trumbull Avenue. The crowd's thunderous roar rocked the stadium and surrounding neighborhood. Motown was spinning and singing. Gibby had just cooked the Goose. The mental image of the Spartan circling the bases, jumping, both arms above his head cannot ever be forgotten. Tigers were ahead again, this time for good 8–4.

Fittingly, it seemed, the last Padre to bat was its all-time greatest player, Tony Gwynn, a Hall of Fame member with well over 3,000 hits and a lifetime batting average of .338. Hernandez coaxed him to fly out to end the game. The Tigers had won the Championship. The Padres lost their first World Series and have not won one since.

Native son, Kirk Gibson, had framed the win with his homers in the first and eighth innings. In this game, in four turns at bat, he had scored three runs and drove in five runs. Tiger shortstop, future Tiger Manager, and Hall of Famer Alan Trammell was voted MVP of the series for hitting .450, two homers, and six RBIs. To this day I personally do not understand the selection. I guess it could have gone to either player.

The frontpage headline in next morning's *Detroit Free Press*, with its one word, said it best:

"G-R-R-R-EAT!"

This World Series ending Sunday was my last day at work in Detroit. The next day, we were transferred back to corporate headquarters in New York. This meant more work, new responsibilities, and another house— but wow, what a way to go!

CHAPTER 7

CHAPTER 8

6TH INNING - BATTLE OF THE BLIMPS

October 23, 1996

In the 1990s, my business partner Phil Lauria and I had the good fortune to meet and collaborate with great clients. Operating out of a modest office in Wilton, Connecticut, our management consulting firm specialized in developing sales and marketing solutions for companies in the consumer goods industry. Our clients ranged in shape and size, including food manufacturers; marketers of health and beauty aids, private label vendors; retailers; sales agencies; public, private, and global corporations; companies in the service, telecommunications, and technology sectors; federal agencies; and consulting firms. Hewlett-Packard, Campbell Soup Company, AT&T, Cadbury Schweppes, and Black & Decker are some examples. The diversity was challenging, the work stimulating. These projects became opportunities to work closely with many great people, building new and energizing connections.

The official mission of LC&A was "Developing and Putting Strategy into Action and Practice." Each engagement was a new, unscripted adventure. We did not bring a prebuilt consulting system or cookie-cutter advisory template. In each case, we customized and devised a fresh roadmap only after the client clearly crystallized their immediate goal or strategic need.

One such client was Philips Electronics, a multi-billion-dollar, multinational, Dutch conglomerate. While driving down to our introductory meeting in their North American headquarters in Stamford, Connecticut, we instinctively assumed that there was an issue or need in one of the product categories—electric shavers, electric toothbrushes, television sets, or compact discs. Or maybe it was the lightbulbs? As we negotiated the twists and turns of the Merritt Parkway, we took mental inventory of our personal households.

But no. This was not going to be about any of those.

This first acquaintance was with an incubator team with a new venture, TradeMedia.net. The group was smart, young, visionary, and were focused on a new business service that was far from the next breakthrough lighting or dental device.

The best I can recollect is that the "world wide web" officially opened for business in 1995, when it was legalized for commercial usage in the United States. Today's meeting occurred in early 1996.

From a personal standpoint, I recall America Online (AOL) breaking new ground when I got my first email address and began hearing, often: "You've Got Mail!" Customers signed up by receiving a compact disc in the mail. Their subscribers reached one million in 1995. The US population was 266 million at the time.

We were the team's first industry prospect. As the Philips group eagerly presented to us, we quickly realized this new venture was one of connecting business to business, not marketing to the consumer.

The concept was to introduce, market, install, manage, and maintain a new service via a new "intranet," linking buyers and sellers of products or services in separate office locations. The users would be enabled to share files, videos, documents, and even meet via video and audio on a confidential basis—in 1996! Hopefully, the economics of it all would work out, following in the footsteps of the Bell Telephone Company.

The retail food sector was the entry market for one reason: it was huge. The industry was comprised of a copious number of suppliers, retailers, and distributors. The larger companies, like Procter & Gamble, Pepsi, Kroger, and Safeway, operated via regional and district offices, sprawled across the country in the markets in which they competed, which were mostly everywhere. The business model was one of high volume, low profit.

Meetings and negotiations were frequent. If this new service could make it here, it could make it anywhere.

Eventually branded the "Super Market Trade Network," (SMTN) the operation was 100 percent functional from the start. The platform (though, it's unclear to me if the concept or term of a "platform" even existed yet) linked all the required component parts—cameras, personal desktop computers, monitors, hardware, proprietary software, and telephone service. To be clear here, this was not Zoom, FaceTime or Skype. This was 1996. (It takes time for technology to reach a tipping point. Video conferencing was the required rage during the COVID-19 Pandemic, but we were doing video conferencing 20+ years ago. While Skype was popular, it was still a decade after we were using video conferencing).

We were quickly hired, after which we advised, designed, and created an industry communication and go-to market strategy: we would focus on message, benefits, pricing, and potential users. During this process, Philips came to understand that we possessed not only industry knowledge, but also industry contacts. We then were further engaged to contact companies to schedule introductory presentations and demonstration meetings. This we accomplished quite often.

We were all laboring diligently and traveling extensively, trunks of demo equipment always in tow. On one early October morning, I found myself on a Delta Airlines flight destined for Atlanta, departing from LaGuardia Airport. As our aircraft took off, the sun still had not yet made its daily appearance. The passenger seated beside me was this trip's client's representative, a young Brit named Declan Dickens. I assumed he was living large in Manhattan.

We were traveling to meet with executives of the Georgia Pacific Company the same afternoon. Safely strapped in, my focus was on that next meeting, the paper industry, and the next sale. Armed with pen in hand I earnestly made notes upon my yellow legal pad on my coffee-stained tray table.

I casually looked up for just a second. After a short gaze, I noticed a couple of nearby New York Yankees caps, here and there. Securing a needed fourth cup of coffee, I surveyed the cabin further. The coffee was dark, but then the realization became clear: we were among a sea of over 50 Yankees caps.

I snatched the *New York Daily News*, which was lying crunched in a seat pocket in the aisle across from me. Suddenly, just then, I realized that today was the fourth game of the World Series. The New York Yankees, already in Atlanta, were pitted against the hometown Braves in Fulton County Stadium, tonight! How had I forgotten? Man, was I working too hard.

After a momentary thought (or, rather, a nanosecond-long thought), I leaned over to my young traveling compatriot. While he peered out the window into the newly blue sky and white clouds, I asked, "Declan, if I was able to procure tickets for us for tonight's World Series baseball game, would you want to go with me instead of that great steak place we planned?" I pointed to the headlines.

Declan viewed the tabloid, over his glasses and paused for a suspenseful while. He replied, "Certainly. We root for the Yankees, right?" Happily securing buy-in, I responded simply, "Certainly!"

Now on to another objective, and as soon as we land (no WiFi): tickets.

Behind two of their three Hall of Fame starting pitchers, John Smoltz and Greg Maddux, the Braves had already blanked the Yanks in the first two games. The opening contests had mercifully ended in the Bronx, but in an embarrassing fashion by the piled-on aggregate score of 16–1.

Thankfully, New York did get one game back, just yesterday, behind the pitching of David Cone and the hitting of Bernie Williams. With Atlanta now leading the series 2 to 1, another Bravo victory will send the Bombers headed back to the Bronx, facing the option of either not losing one more time or facing the pressure of cleaning out their lockers.

Our business meeting went well, but will they buy? I did. I located an industrious purveyor of two stubs in the lobby of the downtown Marriott.

We were able to arrive at the park prior to first pitch. This afforded Declan and me time to become acclimated and leisurely enjoy our gourmet ballpark hot dog dinner. Our expensive but distant roost positioned us well above, but behind home plate. Traditionally, in a World Series game, seat location is of no significant import, as long as it was inside the ballpark. With the lack of a southern chill here, it did not really feel much like a Fall Classic. There was an autumn breeze occasionally blowing out, into the outfield.

The game got under way and started out as a laugher. Jumping out to a 6–0 lead, the Braves chased Yankees starter Kenny Rogers out of the contest by the fifth inning. Of course, this was not Kenny the American singer, songwriter, and chicken-chain entrepreneur. This Kenny was the journeyman pitcher who had played 20 years and accumulated 200 wins—just not *one* in postseason action. (The former was born in Texas and died in Georgia; the latter was born in Georgia and first played in Texas (Rangers).)

The game was not very stimulating, especially for the many New York rooters. I was explaining to Declan how baseball was different from cricket, which he knew everything about and I none, and vice versa. The conversation was drifting on to a comparative discussion of American football vs. rugby, which Declan played in school. It was a grand time, in a "global sports" kind of way. I am not sure if I had mentioned the historic accomplishment of Henry Aaron's 715th record home run. If not, it was admittedly a grand omission on my part, considering the stadium's location in the deep south.

Then came the seventh inning stretch, Declan's first. By this point, Atlanta's lead had diminished, down now to 6–3, but not achieved through terribly exciting play. The Yanks pecked away, assisted by errant Brave fielding and aided by lucky umpire field positioning. Still, just two more innings to go. If the Braves held on, they would go to sleep knowing that they would be just one game away from their first World Championship here in Atlanta, the third in their third city (Boston in 1914 and Milwaukee in 1957, the latter with Aaron).

At the end of the home seventh inning, fans headed to the parking lots. Atlanta fans shuffled off in droves to their cars, racing home to beat the traffic on the overburdened highway. The surrounding area was still under the siege of residual construction from this past summer's Olympic Games.

I was appalled. Suddenly it seemed as though 25 percent of the seats in the stadium had become unoccupied. This was the World Series, for God's sake. What about the celebration at the end of the game, watching the final out? What if something great or rare happens, like a triple play, a grand slam home run, or a thrilling, acrobatic, game saving catch. *What?* I would be in the car listening to it on the radio?! *Never!* (On one future day, these are words I would have to swallow).

CHAPTER 8

As I was in the process of explaining to Declan the why and the how of such a historic travesty, the Yankees were brewing a rally. In the top of the eighth inning, Manager Bobby Cox (Cox was a Yankee himself once, in his only two years as a player in the majors) summoned into the game their closer, Mark Wohlers, who promptly relinquished two base hits. However, it looked as though he was about to escape his self-created jam. Yankee Mariano Duncan hit a routine double-play ground ball, botched by the shortstop. This unfortunate incident afforded an extra out, an additional at bat for New York. The batter was the recently inserted catcher, Jim Leyritz, now in his second turn at bat. Manager Joe Torre had made the switch a few innings earlier (Torre was a Brave for the first half of his 18-year playing career).

To the deafening hush of the residual Braves faithfuls—and the cheers of the traveling Yankees fans—Leyritz crashed a deep, three-run homer over the centerfield fence. Instantaneously, the game was tied 6–6! The game was no longer enjoyable to most of the present fans *or* to those riding home, listening in their cars.

No scoring by either side in the final inning then led to New York winning in an extra and tenth inning, aided by their opposition—their two runs were scored by the benefit of a bases-loaded walk and a fielding error. The Yankees eventually held on to a win by the score of 8–6. This victory marked the team's largest comeback in its exceptionally long and storied World Series history. A new, young player named Derek Jeter scored the final run.

Back in their comfortable Bronx home, the Yankees finished off the Braves, sweeping them in the next two games in the House that Ruth Built.

Surprisingly, Joe Torre had won his first World Series championship. He had managed for 14 years in the National League for the New York Mets, the Braves, and the St. Louis Cardinals, finishing first only once (that team was swept in the 1982 NLCS—it was these Braves).

His first year in the American League was the charm, and it became much more than that. The Yankees had started off on another championship team run, and this core team won three more championships in the next four years. Brooklyn native Torre managed the Yankees for 12 more consecutive seasons.

Four years before writing this, I asked Declan if he remembered attending this game. He replied, "I have never forgotten, Pat! Especially the battle of the blimps hovering over the stadium—CNN and FOX, with battling messages from Ted Turner and Rupert Murdoch!"

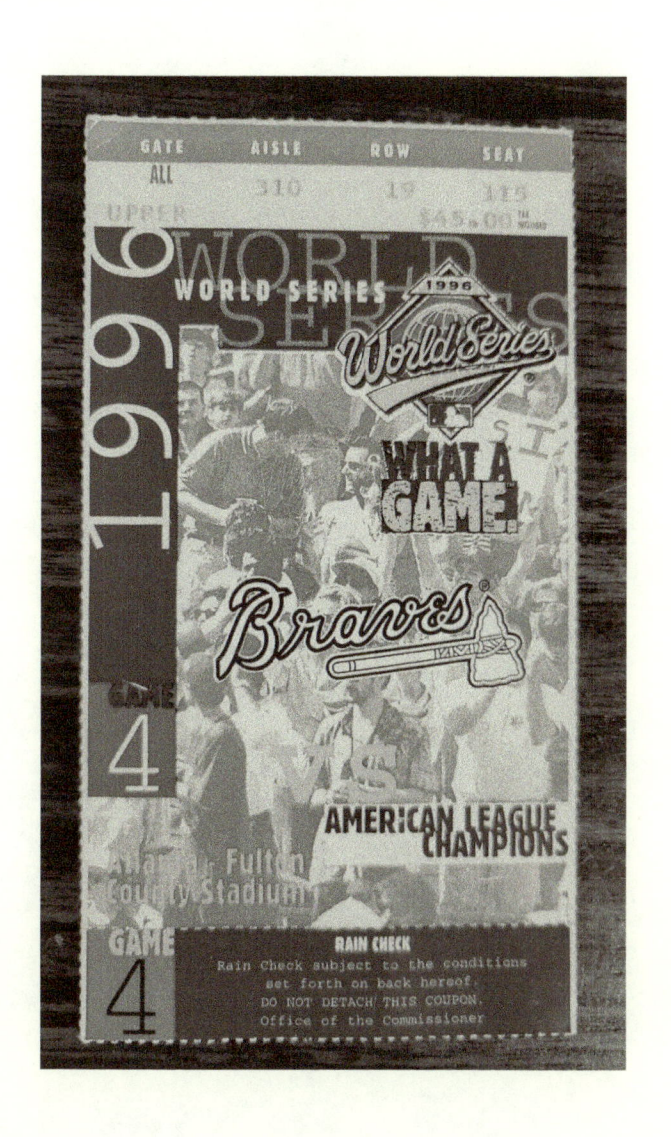

CHAPTER 8

CHAPTER 9

7TH INNING - NEW YORK MINUTE

September 21, 2001

Will anyone ever forget exactly where they were and exactly what they were doing on September 11, 2001?

I was in Las Vegas, at the MGM Grand Hotel, and I was attending the International Baking Industry Exposition (IBIE). I was leading national sales for a large, family-owned, baked goods company. I arrived over the previous weekend, and we had been on green fairways and entertaining our customers nightly. During the day, we either were walking the trade show floor, conducting planning sessions with supermarket bakery buyers, or managing sales meetings.

Early in the morning, I was attempting to tidy up the day's meeting room. My suite served as a station to entertain customers after dinner the prior evening—or, I should more accurately say, earlier this same morning. I was thinking about our always interesting meeting with one of our customers, this one based in Bentonville, Arkansas, in this same room yesterday. I had an upcoming conference call with New York District Sales Manager, Lenny D'Andrea, to discuss our usual business issue concerning our largest customer in that market.

I dialed. Before I could say, "Good morning," I quickly had a feeling that it was not going to be one.

Lenny said, "Pat, I cannot believe what I am looking at. Turn on your TV!"

I did. Like so many others, together we watched the second plane go into the second Tower, as stunned as the rest of the world.

In Las Vegas, like most everywhere else, we became a part of the nationwide stoppage after the attack. The sky was closed. No planes were flying, no trains or buses were running, no car rentals were available, no telephone or cellular service, no nothing—not a thing. All was shut down and put on pause.

We were an action-oriented group, always in motion—partly due to our sales DNA and also likely due to our collective ADHD. Expectedly, after two days of standing still, three of us voted to drive a rental car across the country. Others did likewise—even a Major League Baseball Hall of Famer.

While writing this tale the author read dozens of books on the subject of baseball. While this was intend-

CHAPTER 9

ed for inspiration and research, sometimes my reading exceeded my writing. One book which caught my interest was a revealing biography on the late, great Ernie Banks, authored by Ron Rapoport in 2019: *Let's Play Two*. The book opens with a short prologue, *Omaha*.

On 9/11 Ernie was at a Warren Buffet meeting and golf event in Nebraska. After three days of waiting around, Banks and another friend located a vehicle to rent. The two then headed out on their seven-hour ride back to Chicago. Throughout his life, unlike most sports superstars, Banks rarely talked about himself or about his remarkable personal journey (his youth in Dallas, excelling with the Kansas City Monarchs in the Negro League, being the first player to break the color line for the Chicago Cubs in 1953, playing all 19 years with that same team without ever playing in a World Series game, the agonizing 1969 regular season, being Mr. Cub at all times and forever, etc.). I personally watched him play, especially in 1969. Always carrying a smile, he was smooth in the field, prolific, and clutch at the plate, especially inside Wrigley Field. I was not the only one to feel that way about him. Ernie Banks became a first ballot member of Cooperstown and was a delight to watch.

Let's Play Two brings to light that he was also complicated.

On the long drive, with all the time in the world and no one else in the room, Banks opened up about everything to his riding companion. After hours of fascinating conversation, they stopped to ask for directions—and should have sooner. They had been traveling along the South Dakota grasslands in the wrong direction and were closing in on North Dakota, the last state between them and another country. Their seven-hour drive had taken them to the mistaken north instead of the intended east.

Over a thousand miles west of Omaha, Bill Nolan also located one such vehicle, luckily rented for the past weekend's meeting on the golf course.

We commenced our long drive out of the Mojave Desert. We made sure we headed east. With dual destinations set for North Carolina and Connecticut, we charted a path via the ancient byway, Route 66, sometimes labeled Interstate 40. The road and weather were clear. Alternating, Bill, Mike Brown, and I drove through day and night, sharing ownership of the controls and the wheel. We paused for one three-hour break and shower at a roadside motel, which was approximately located in Amarillo, Texas. The MGM Grand it was not.

While stationed in the backseat, I remember being finally able to connect my mobile phone with Sprint or AT&T. I listened to a faint, unclear voicemail message, over and over. It was from my sister. Anna resides in lower Manhattan, less than 30 blocks away from Ground Zero (yet she was checking in on me!). She was also wondering about the status of our cousin, Bernard.

CHAPTER 9

He sold government securities for Cantor Fitzgerald, his desk located in company offices above the 100th Floor in Tower 1. Bern was, tragically, one of the company's 658 who never returned home from work that day.

Our company travel agent, late in the morning of the second day, told us commercial airlines had begun to operate again. Seats were available. The skies were open for business. After a 1,100-mile drive, crossing the Continental Divide, and with just one talked-away speeding violation to our credit, we set out to our new target destination. The nearest major airport was in Oklahoma City. The irony did not escape us. The city was the site of the last domestic terror attack, just five years earlier.

Our riding adventure concluded with our fleecing by United Airlines. UA charged $1,000 for a new ticket—and the right to board a virtually empty aircraft. One of us has never flown United again. The other two use it as a dead last resort. Despite this, we were more than thankful to be curtailing our scenic cross-country tour. After eventually locating my car at Hartford Airport, I was happy to be back home with family and still unable to make sense of it all.

Outside the New York area, most people would not be aware that Shea Stadium in Queens functioned as a staging area. New Yorkers knew. First responders and supplies regularly dispatched from the baseball park's portside location on Flushing Bay. Supply-stocked craft passed by Riker's Island as they made their way down the East River to lower Manhattan and Ground Zero. Manager Bobby Valentine and the New York Met organization were doing their part in the recovery effort.

Valentine tells a story of one night when a gang of Hells Angels bikers showed up, pulling up to the barricades. He did not know what to expect. The leader said that they had heard on the radio that the Mets needed help. They were there to pitch in. The two teams silently worked side by side, loading boats. With the night's job completed, the motorcycle band quietly sped away. During that crisis, *everyone* pulled together.

Baseball, like most everything in the country, was on pause, the season suspended—similarly, they are also suspended during the time of this writing in 2020. The country eventually set out on its attempt to get back to "normal." Major League Baseball returned to play on September 17, but not in New York City.

Ten days after that horrific day, the city scheduled its first public event. It was to be a baseball game. The first professional sports team to play in New York were to be the Mets at Shea Stadium. I always looked forward to its home run, the Big Apple rising on the other side of the right center field wall. It only arose for Met home runs, not those of the visiting team. The opponent would be their perennial rival, the first-place Atlanta Braves. This was appropriate on so many levels.

CHAPTER 9

My company held a Mets partial-season ticket plan. These two seats had become particularly handy in the previous year when the Mets squared off against the New York Yankees in the first NY Subway Series since 1956.

Leaving our safe cover in the Connecticut woods behind, we set out for this historic game on September 21st. We cautiously traversed the usual 60-minute path to the game along Connecticut Route #15, the chaotic highway with multiple identities. Depending on where you were located, it might be the Wilbur Cross Highway, the Merritt Parkway, or the Hutchinson River Parkway. Its importance, however, was not its name but that it led to the bridge and to the Whitestone Expressway into Flushing.

Associate Route 66 driver, Mike, accompanied me. On this unusually traffic-free Friday night ride, we discussed the situation soon coming upon us. We concluded that we had absolutely no idea what to expect, except, eventually, a baseball game. We dined traditionally at the Parkside Restaurant in Corona. We then creatively located a parking space which was not located inside the stadium parking lot. This coveted curbside spot also happened to be located just 5000 feet from the author's first purchased house in Jackson Heights. The unattached red brick house nestled across the street from a row of landing lights which assisted the pilot's approach to LaGuardia Airport.

Like the planes, we crossed the Grand Central Parkway over a little known and very narrow pedestrian bridge. We ambled along the promenade past the point where Skyline Cruise tour boats usually were docked; they were now replaced by recovery vessels and police boats. Then we went under the Northern Boulevard overpass and across the large stadium parking lot, which was surrounded by floodlights, police cruisers, and military vehicles.

It was strange, eerie, confusing; instead of the usual pregame hubbub we had barricades, police cars, military, metal detectors, and wands. Long, quiet, slow lines at the gates admitted uncertain and apprehensive fans.

Then suddenly, out of the blue (and orange), I recognized a familiar face—from childhood, no less, from elementary school and even Cub Scouts, and now—I also know—a Mets fan. On one of the outfield lines was Ronnie Bloch! Seeing Ron and shaking his hand for the first time in 25 years was at least one familiar moment of comfort...of a sort.

I had not seen Ron[1] since his wedding day in 1975. While en route to the event at the San Roc Café in Yonkers, driving via the Major Deegan Expressway, I had

---

1   If it was not for this book's research, I would not have known that Ron passed away in 2019, after selling his NY CPA firm, moving to Florida, and pursuing his passion of teaching and becoming the Principal at Holy Trinity Episcopal School which provides programs and support for students with learning difficulties. RIP Ronnie.

CHAPTER 9

crashed my first General Foods company car. The large maroon Matador sedan (American Motors Corporation) was not really a thing of beauty, neither before nor after the smash. I deposited its front end into the trunk of a car with New Jersey license plates whose driver, driving exactly like one from said state, had cut over at the last second to catch the exit ramp to the George Washington Bridge. It was just 1000 feet past Yankee Stadium, in front of the Stadium Motor Lodge.

At the game, we uneasily waited in our seats, located in the upper deck behind home plate. The usual LaGuardia air traffic noise added to the tension; fans often looked up to keep track of the trails of the planes. The game's pregame ceremony was long, special, and emotional—must-see YouTube TV. The US Marines performed a 21-gun salute, the NY Police Department bagpipes played *Amazing Grace,* Diana Ross sang *God Bless America,* and New York's Marc Anthony sang *The Star-Spangled Banner.* Locating a dry eye among the over 41,000 in attendance was an impossible task. Mike recently reminded me that I never removed my sunglasses all night at this night game.

Then opposing players crossing the lines embraced. The Mets wore caps of Police, Fire, EMS, and Military in honor of the fallen and still committed. Fellow Jasper alum, Mayor Rudy Giuliani, on this particular day, cheered.

The game commenced—baseball was back, and meaningful baseball was back: my Metropolitans versus their archrival and nemesis, Atlanta Braves, who they trailed by only five-and-a-half games in the Division standings. Led by Manager Bobby Cox, the team included a cadre of future Hall of Fame players, with Chipper Jones and the pitching trio of Tom Glavine, John Smoltz, and Greg Maddux. The former ended up hitting forty-nine of his 468 career home runs against the Mets, the threesome winners of seven Cy Young Awards.

The game on the field was a tense, seesaw affair. A pitcher's duel developed between Mets Bruce Chen and Braves Jason Marquis, the latter originally from Staten Island. The seventh inning stretch, punctuated by an unforgettable rendition of *New York, New York* by Liza Minelli, saw the score tied 1–1.

In the top of the eighth inning, Mets relief pitcher John Franco, also from Staten Island, found himself in trouble that usual closer, Armando Benitez, could not get him out of. The Mets and their crowd now found themselves trailing 2–1.

In the bottom of the inning the Braves brought in relief pitcher Steve Karsay who ended up having 20 saves this year. Karsay was born in Flushing and was drafted into the majors from Christ the King High School in Queens, only five miles away. CTK was also the school that my lost cousin Bern had attended.

The inning started out quietly and quickly enough with a groundout. But then, Edgardo Alfonso worked his turn into a walk. At this point, the crowd began stirring, cheering, and chanting. Valentine inserted speedster Desi Relaford in as a pinch runner. I remember thinking, hoping, that maybe the Mets could manufacture a run here, tie the game, and make the bottom of the ninth more interesting—tying runner on, only one out, only one run behind. This was a reasonable possibility, especially with future Hall of Famer Mike Piazza coming up to bat.

We did not have to wait until the next inning.

The former Dodger and twelve-time All-Star catcher connected on Karsay's second offering. With a distinctively loud crack of the bat, Piazza sent the pitch on its long, magical ride. As the ball kept carrying, Golden Glove center fielder, Andruw Jones, kept chasing. Only when the ball hit the camera pavilion did we all know it was gone. The crowd was instantly quieted, stunned—then they immediately erupted into a long, deafening roar and release. The stadium was shaking, American flags were waving, there were smiles and more tears. Something incredibly moving *and* positive had just happened in New York City, if only for a minute.

You knew that even the Braves in the losing dugout wanted to cheer. Years later, Chipper said that he had expected Piazza to hit the dramatic home run. He also said that it was the only time, ever, that he was okay with the opposing team winning. After calling the epic home run, broadcaster Harry Rose stated it well: "Shea Stadium has something to smile about."

With the Braves starting a rally, ninth inning theatrics followed, which quieted the crowd, now again on edge. Then a smashed ball to the shortstop, skillfully converted into a bang-bang, game-ending double play. The Mets had survived 3–2, prompting the fans off the edge of their seats again, then down through the exit ramps, cheering "U! S! A!" and, "Let's Go Mets!" just as they had been all night long.

Upon his 2016 induction into Cooperstown, Piazza said that of all his 427 career dingers (396 as a catcher, the most in baseball history), that this one in September 2001, was his most important. This lucky fan, who watched the baseball fly over the wall to see the Big Apple rise again on that unforgettable night in Queens, could not agree any more.

CHAPTER 9

CHAPTER 10

8TH INNING - TRIBORO TOLL

October 31 and November 1, 2001

In New York, 9/11-postponed Major League Baseball started with the Mets at Shea Stadium (see *7th Inning*). The season came to its end in Yankee Stadium - with the city's other team.

The Yankees had won 95 games in the regular season, a .594 winning percentage—but this was not the highest in the league. In the playoffs, they had survived two showdowns in the West. They outlasted the Oakland Athletics in the AL Division Series and beat the Seattle Mariners in the AL Championship Series, winners of 102 and 116 games, respectively. They were set to represent the American League in the 2001 World Series, remarkably for the 38th time in their team history. The NL opponent was to be the four-years young Diamondbacks of Arizona, clearly an expansion team.

This was their first turn (their presence in the Series has not been repeated since).

Recently the Bronx Bombers had been on one of their many championship rolls. In this era, they had won four of the last five World Championships, commencing in 1996 (see *6th Inning*). At least New York had something small yet positive to think about.

Twenty-five years later (see *2nd Inning*), another chance to witness a championship game at Yankee Stadium came my way. This time the invitation came from Mike Myers. Mike was a new friend, great business partner, and a lifelong Yankees fan, originally from Minneapolis but raised in Connecticut. His favorite player is the late Thurman Munson. The Yankees catcher was on the field during my other Bronx championship experience in 1976. Remember that one ending with the epic walk off home run (not 1951)? Munson became both the Yankee Captain and the American League's Most Valuable Player in that pennant-winning season.

More recently though, Mike had been quick to admit that Derek Jeter, The Captain, was quickly catching up to his favorite frontrunner. In just the previous year, 2000, Jeter was the Most Valuable Player in both the American League Championship Series (ALCS) and in the Subway Series against the Mets.

The official business request was to join Mike and two bakery customers who were employees of the Great A&P Company—a curious corporate moniker, since they were not really great (average, at best) and are nonexistent today. A more compelling question is how two executives from A&P are mentioned for a second time in this book.

The primetime game's start time was great for FOX Sports but created a scheduling issue for me. On the very next morning I was to be sitting at a conference table at eight o'clock. That room was located at the corporate headquarters of Denny's Restaurants in Spartanburg, South Carolina. How was I to accomplish both experiencing World Series baseball and doing my job?

Creative problem solving quickly hatched a plan:

(1.) Drive down from Connecticut to Yankee Stadium in the Bronx.

(2.) Post game, drive to and sleep quickly in a LaGuardia airport hotel in Queens.

(3.) Catch the next morning's first flight out to Greenville, South Carolina.

Not perfect, but theoretically plausible and logistically sound.

World Series Game # 4 was to be played in The House That Ruth Built in the 20s, remodeled in the 70s. Today's date was October 31. Yes, for the first time ever, baseball was to be played on Halloween. Above us the stadium lights burned brightly in the autumn air. Beyond them was baseball's giant jack-o-lantern—eerily, the full moon glowed brighter. What would the candy companies be merchandising if this had been normal timing? Chocolate baseball pumpkins, candy-corn-filled bats, orange-and-black favorite player jerseys, goblin baseball caps? I should have asked our guest buyers. I may have asked but have forgotten their answer.

Arizona had captured the first two games of the series, both played indoors in the desert. The pitching duo of Kurt Schilling and the *Big Unit,* Randy Johnson, was formidable. The Yanks scored just one run, managed only six hits, and struck out 20 times in the two games. New York did get one back yesterday behind the strong pitching of Roger Clemens and Mariano Rivera in the third game. Schilling was to pitch again tonight.

The crowd quietly absorbed the singing of the National Anthem, collectively providing solemn respect to the police officers and first responders whose presence was recognized by perennial public address announcer, Bob Sheppard (Sheppard, born and raised in Queens, was the stadium's familiar and elegant voice for over 50 years, living for four months shy of 100 years of age). As it had been at every game played since his first one (in 1951), Sheppard's voice was revered and referred to as the Voice of God.

It was nearly November and it was chilly, but it was championship baseball in Yankee Stadium. That is how it was supposed to be and feel. From high above and behind home plate, we admired the work of dueling pitchers, Schilling and Yank starter, *El Duque,* Orlando Hernandez.

CHAPTER 10

The D-Backs eventually developed a lead. The Yanks fought back. There was a breeze, it was getting colder, the game—with all its television commercials—dragged on. Our guests from the Great A&P evacuated, fleeing to their homes in New Jersey at the end of the eighth inning and to get a jump on the brutal postgame traffic onto the George Washington Bridge.

The Diamondbacks had broken a tense tie with two runs in the top of the inning. The Yankees failed to respond in their half. They did not impress while trying. Arizona's relief ace, Byung-Hyun Kim, was executing well. The sidearm submarine thrower from South Korea had mowed them down, striking out the side, three up, three down—and the game was now down to its final three outs. I can understand the premature departure of our guests. However, as we have learned, you are not supposed to leave an unfinished World Series game.

Mike and I stayed the course, hanging in there, Yanks still trailing 3–1, preparing for their last bat. We endured more long commercial breaks, though it was now well after 11:00 p.m. It was already an over-three-hour game, closing in on four hours of real time.

I looked over to the loyal Yankees fan, saying, "Hey Mike, I really have to go. I have to get in my bed for a few minutes before I board my airplane."

His drive back home to Glastonbury, Connecticut was over 100 miles. Tacitly understanding the magnitude of our decision, breaking the uncodified rule of exiting a World Series game before its conclusion, Mike agreed.

We headed down the exit ramps to the street. Mike and I were just about to take our next and last step out of the stadium into the cold Bronx night when we heard the roar of the crowd. We stopped and looked up at the television monitor above the concession stand in front of us. The Yankees had a base runner on first with two outs. We stood in place to watch the final strike or out.

Except that it was not.

New York first-baseman, Tino (DBA Tippy) Martinez, hit the first pitch thrown to him, deep into the right center field stands. The game was tied, now 3–3! The stadium, still full of Yankees faithful, was now in a state of frenzy. Stunned, like all of Arizona, Mike and I looked at each other. Should we head back to our seats? After all, it was now a new game. The Yankees might even still win it here, still in their last turn at bat. Once again, we agreed to stay the course and decided again to get on the road—one, the diehard Yankee fan, the other, the lifelong baseball fan. We departed.

For that decision, we, together, would pay the ultimate price.

With no crowds—why would anyone leave an unfinished World Series game?—I was able to easily retrieve my strategically parked rental car. I set out on the 10-minute drive over the bridge to the Airport

CHAPTER 10

Marriott, tuning into the game's radio broadcast. As I coasted along the empty Major Deegan Expressway, I was thinking, "how could I?" Yet, I was still not believing that I had seen Tino's game-tying blast on a television monitor, despite being inside the ballpark.

I was intently tracking the contest—the Yankees were actually coming close to winning it in that ninth inning but didn't. Arizona then went down 1–2–3 - in order in the top of the tenth, their three ground ball outs induced by The Sandman and closer, Rivera.

Kim was still pitching, now his third inning of relief. He got the first two outs, both fly balls to the outfield. At least the Yanks were now making contact, no longer whiffing.

Derek Jeter came up to bat. So far, in four games, Jeter had managed one lone hit in his sixteen at bats. Officially, he was batting .063 for the series. After the first pitch, the radio announcer welcomed everyone to "Baseball in November", as the clock had just then struck midnight. The full moon was still in observance, but no longer could we claim the day or night as Halloween. It was November, for the first time in baseball history.

Jeter fought, fouling off pitch after pitch. Aided by Kim's three outside pitches, the two battled to a full count. It was now up to an eighth pitch at bat. I was just now on the eighth minute of my drive to a quick sleep.

I am not sure where Mike's car was when it happened. I assume he was somewhere between Yonkers and White Plains. I had just pulled up to the toll booth gates of the Triboro Bridge.

As I was dropping my eight quarters into the basket in order to gain exit from the Bronx and entry into Queens, I could not believe my ears. Like the previous two batters, Jeter hit a fly ball—only his sailed over the fence in right field. The shortstop had hit a walk off home run to win, 4–3! Mike and I had missed witnessing the instantaneous birth of *Mr. November*.

The celebrating Yankees were off to their clubhouse showers and then on to their happy rides home. They were playing again soon in Game #5, on this new, same day. I was off to South Carolina, much sooner, but somehow still grateful.

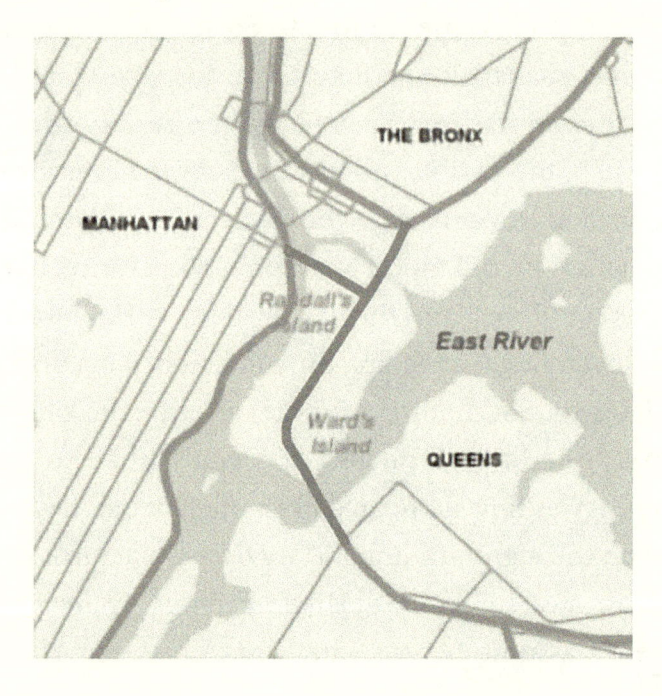

CHAPTER 11

9TH INNING - "YA GOTTA BELIEVE!"

October 27, 2019

We were blessed to be still living and also residing in Washington, DC on Capitol Hill—regardless of what you may think. After over 30 years, we moved out of our spacious, 1983, New England-style saltbox, nestled in the Connecticut woods. We now resided in a cozy, 1905, Federal-style row house stationed 13 blocks from the "Hill," the US Supreme Court, and the National Mall—and a 20-minute jog to Washington Nationals Park (a baseball stadium).

Much more importantly, we were now situated just five short city blocks from our daughter, Tina, and our three beautiful grandkids. This meant Little League, soccer, dance recitals, backyard Sunday BBQs, school picnics, sleepovers, birthdays, museum visits, Halloween—and Washington Nationals baseball games.

Tina and her husband Will had been living in Washington for quite a while, even before they both finished law school and certainly considerably before Major League Baseball decided to return to the city.

Washington politics is confusing, complex, convoluted, and sometimes shut down. The history of Washington professional baseball is not dissimilar and may eclipse it—minimally, the latter gives the former a run for its money. Read and decide for yourself.

Today's Washington Nationals compete in the East Division of the National League. They are the reincarnated Montreal Expos, which legally immigrated to the District of Columbia. The Expos were Major League Baseball's first foreign team, established via the league's 1969 expansion and named after *Expo 67*, one of the most successful World Fairs, which was held in Canada's centennial year. The author fondly recalls attending the exhibition in the spring of 1967, after what, for a kid, seemed like an endless train ride from New York City.

This coincided with the dawn of divisional play with which the new team had good success. The Expos broke through in 1981, taking the eventual World Champion Los Angeles Dodgers to the full five-game limit of the National League Championship Series. They were a talented team in the 80s. Mediocrity then crept in. A managerial change in 1993—which included a father-and-son duo (Manager Felipe Alou and Outfielder Moises Alou)—sparked the team. They were on a tear in 1994 and destined for greatness. Their .649 winning percentage (74 W–40 L) assured that. However, in that year, a players' strike marred the sport. Baseball and the Expos' season unfortunately ended in August. Over the next decade's team performance, fan interest and attendance declined. The franchise was set to fold when Major League Baseball (MLB) took over its ownership. MLB decided that the club required a permanent change in scenery. In 2005, the Expos became today's Washington Nationals.

Growing up in the 50s and 60s, I recall Washington baseball as always being the Senators and always being in last place in the American League. It was a destination city. A player was either traded or a manager hired at the end or *to* end their career. It was baseball's purgatory, preceding retirement.

Since 1971, there had been no professional baseball played in the nation's Capital. Reflectively, this seemed downright un-American.

The original (first) Washington Senators played for 95 years, until 1961, when they abandoned town. They transferred to the Twin Cities where they became the Minnesota Twins in an expansion of the American League, along with the Los Angeles Angels and a third team—in Washington, DC. The league and its owners struck a deal (a common occurrence). In this same year, the league replaced the first Senators with a new (second) Senator team. The change did not change anything on the field of play. The new club played just as badly. This second Senator team played in the city a mere ten years, then they also left, relocating to Arlington (and I don't mean Virginia). They became the Texas Rangers in 1971.

Understanding all that is as simple as passing a bill in Congress, or throwing a ball to first base—right?

The original (first) Senators did win one World Series in 1924—pretty close to a century ago from this writing. I found the managers, at the time of these transitions, to be noteworthy.

A man named Cookie Lavagetto was the Senator manager since 1957; he led the initial exodus in 1961. By definition—and likely by airplane—Cookie became the first manager of the Minnesota Twins. Cookie had played seven years with the Brooklyn Dodgers. His first year as Dodger bench coach was 1951, which should be a familiar year to the reader by now.

A New York photographer caught Lavagetto forever in a post-game newspaper photo at the end of that Dodger season. His impossible task was to console a crying pitcher, Ralph Branca—the Dodger guilty forever of throwing the pitch for a home run by Bobby Thompson, the *Shot Heard 'Round the Baseball World* (see *Batting Practice*). It is unclear how effective he was in this effort. In the photographed scene, Branca was literally lying face down, sprawled across the clubhouse stairs.

CHAPTER 11

A picture is worth a thousand words. Lavagetto's facial expression stands as great testimony to this aged adage.

In 1971, the second Senator team's manager was also a former player, this one much more famous than Cookie—a fellow named Ted Williams. Similarly, by leading the second evacuation to Dallas, Williams became the first manager of the new Texas Rangers.

In 2005, the Expos' Manager who led their international journey from Montreal to the District of Columbia was none other than Frank Robinson, and therefore the first manager of the Nationals. At the time, he was working for MLB and was tapped for the job.

While Lavagetto is of curious note (due to the birthdate of the author and the premise of this book), the conjunction of Williams and Robinson is historically more hallowed and holy—in terms of their Hall of Fame playing careers. Consider just these accomplishments:

Ted Williams played for 19 years and only for the Boston Red Sox. His career spanned four decades and two wars, which included five years of military service—a significant subtraction of playing time while still in his prime. In the American League, Williams was a six-time batting champion, voted Most Valuable Player (MVP) twice, accomplished a lifetime batting average of .344, hit 521 career Home Runs, earned a Triple Crown (leader in BA, HRs, and RBIs), and was the last player ever to hit for a batting average of or higher than .400 (.406 in 1941).

A BASEBALL BIRTHRIGHT

Frank Robinson played for 21 years, mostly for the Cincinnati Reds and Baltimore Orioles. His playing career crossed three decades. Robinson was Rookie of the Year (1956),[1] earned a Triple Crown, hit 586 career Home Runs, was a World Series MVP, and, finally, was the Most Valuable Player in *both* leagues—National (1961) and American (1966)—the only player in baseball history *ever* to do so.

Robinson was baseball's first Black manager—in *each* league (1975 AL—Cleveland Indians, 1981 NL—San Francisco Giants) and voted Manager of the Year in 1989 (Baltimore Orioles).

But I digress, and not for the last time, bringing us back to 2019.

The new team's (again, the transferred Montreal Expos) inaugural three seasons (2005–2007) were in the old Robert F. Kennedy (RFK) Football Stadium, the former home to the one-time National Football League Washington Redskins (the RFK is soon to be demolished or redeveloped).

Tina and Will had gone through a string of losing playoff ringers with this new Washington baseball team. Unlike their Senator predecessors, the Nationals

---

[1] Ted Williams was not Rookie of the Year. The recognition did not exist when his career started. The first Rookie of the Year was awarded to a different Robinson, by the name of Jackie, who broke the player color barrier in the same year—1947.

were good. They had already won four Division titles. It took them only until 2012—just seven years—to win their first Division title, then three more followed for a respectable, if not remarkable, total of four within a six-year span.

Inexplicably they somehow (and in so many similar ways) managed not to win one, single, playoff series. It seemed as though it was only in the playoffs that they played like the Senator teams of old.

Most series were excruciating—home playoff game debacles, extra inning affairs, and tight series losses were all witnessed by this young couple. The Nationals never quickly disappeared. For Will, Tina, and the entire Nationals fandom, playoff play was more of a slow bleed. It was the simultaneous case of getting your money's worth and wishing that you never paid.

The first playoff series was an indicator of this future trend. In 2012, while playing the St. Louis Cardinals—that year's eventual World Series Champions—the Nats entered the ninth inning of the final and fifth game of the Division Series with a lead at home. Leading 7–5, they needed to retire just the last three Cards to clinch. Instead, Washington allowed the Cards to fabricate a four-run rally and lost, 9–7.

History notes that the best (or worst) example would be their next crack at it in 2014, against the San Francisco Giants (who were also the eventual World Series Champions). They had already lost the home opener by one run, so Game #2 was critical. Here again, they took a lead—by one run—into the final inning. Now, characteristically, the bullpen allowed the Giants to score a run to tie in the ninth. What transpired next could be the definition of excruciating: *nine innings later*, they had lost again, by the score of 2–1. The 18-inning game, up until that point in time, was the longest playoff game in history in terms of both innings and time, lasting nearly six-and-a-half hours.

Similar NLDS results continued to occur: first in 2016 against the Dodgers, when they lost the fourth and fifth games at home, each by just one run; the scenario replayed in 2017 against the Cubs, when they lost at home again, again in the fifth and final game by one run, 9–8.

Washington National playoff history was exhausting and nothing but pure agony—until this new year of 2019. Ironically and fittingly, the Nationals had snuck into this year's playoffs by winning—rather, qualifying for—the second Wild Card position.

Tina had witnessed the other and better side of all this, once when much younger. Thirty-three years earlier (on October 25th), Tina assumed her mandatory seating location in our Connecticut family room. We were watching the 1986 World Series. The New York Mets were close to losing their chance at winning a world championship. They had just allowed two runs in the top of the tenth inning. We were watching anoth-

CHAPTER 11

er two-out at bat, this one of Game #6—their last batter. Making the out would end the series between my New York Mets and their Boston Red Sox.

The Mets were in the midst of a rally in the tenth inning and had just tied the game on a wild pitch. The superstitious directive came directly from her dad (author) and her grandfather (see *2nd Inning*). The Mets had entered this inning about to be toast in New York while Beantown was ready to toast their Sox as champions. The Curse of the Bambino would finally be broken, and quite a party was probably planned. The city would finally have its first trophy since Babe Ruth's trade to the Yankees in 1919. The Mets were on the edge but had not yet fallen over it. Superstitiously, nothing should change in the room—stay in your seat! *You Gotta Believe!*

The two-out, two-strike at bat incredibly consumed six excruciating minutes. Eventually, a bouncing ground ball off the bat of Mookie Wilson headed toward the right side of Shea Stadium's infield. The slow grounder incredulously traveled through the legs of first baseman Bill Buckner, and rolled, not-so-innocently, into right field. On third base was Ray Knight, who immediately dashed home to score the winning run on the game-ending error. The starting Met pitcher on the next day in Game #7 was Ron Darling, the final game, which the Mets won. Darling had also been the winning pitcher in Game #4.

The Bad Guys won! The Mets were World Champions!

Darling was the first television color commentator of the Nationals in their 2005 inaugural season. Knight was a radio color commentator for the Nationals for 12 years through 2018.

There was this *Met connection* thing here in Washington, at least in the author's imagination. It was exactly 50 years since the '69 *Miracle Mets*. (To catch up on that, I suggest a great new read with a fresh perspective and a great backdrop of the times, Wayne Coffey's 2019 book, *They Said It Could Not Be Done.*)

In this year's exciting Wild Card run, the Nationals had beaten the Milwaukee Brewers in the play-in Wild Card game played in Milwaukee, outlasted the LA Dodgers in five games in the NL Division Series, and swept the St. Louis Cards in the NL Championship Series in four games. They were now on to the first World Series in Washington, DC since 1924.

Just three days earlier the fans and city were really feeling it, collectively giddy. Clear thinking and expectation were that the Nationals might actually sweep the Houston Astros. NATITUDE was in full swing. They were on track to clinch the World Series at home with their three chances to play. After all, they had just won the first two games in Minute Maid Park in Texas.

Only the DMV (DC, MD, VA) populace woke up today to find itself in a real mess and was greeted by a morning of lost momentum. The Astros had tied up the series. The Nationals had lost the first two games

CHAPTER 11

at home. Tina and Will had attended and witnessed the Game #3 defeat, a blowout. A second thrashing followed, with a loss to a substitute minor league pitcher. Championship euphoria transformed into playoff depression.

What else is new?

Later today, Game #5 of the 2019 World Series would be upon us. I felt compelled to act, to do something, anything, to stem this Texas Tide. (In the worst case, I would attend another World Series game.) I eventually found expensive access to three very upper deck tickets. This would be a perfect perch with a birds-eye view. Just a few seats away from the very yellow right field flagpole, the occupants of the three seats were three generations: daughter, grandson, Wynn (see *Bullpen*), with the author watching from afar—literally with the birds and the pigeons.

The DC crowd opened the game by warmly welcoming the honorary first pitch of Chef and Humanitarian José Andrés, an immigrant from Spain and US citizen (the same man who notably backed out of his planned restaurant in the new Trump Hotel). Later in the game, the DC crowd also welcomed the then current President, only not as warmly.

The Nationals were set to face Gerrit Cole. They had already beaten Cole in Game #1, catching him off his game. This night did not go well against the strikeout (326!) king of the American League. The Nationals mustered a mere four hits. The Astros only had six more. Three of them were two-run home runs. Things seemed familiarly bleak at the conclusion of this last game of the year at Nationals Park. The game mercifully ended (7–1) and completed a humbling three home game sweep by the Houston opposition.

Over the past four days the Nationals had played poorly, quite Washington Senator-like, almost as if frozen in time. They were under the pressure of playing in front of their loyal fans, obviously pressing, scoring only one run in each of the three games.

As the crowd provided them with a long and final standing ovation, my daughter looked over to me, saying, "I really don't care if we lose again this year. I am here with my dad and son at a World Series game, and nothing could be better than that."

I replied, "Yes, a wonderful memory—but there are still two more games. You are going back to that band box in Houston, and you have Scherzer and Strasburg pitching. The Nationals are going to win. Ya Gotta Believe!"

Before the series started, I had predicted that the Nats would beat the Astros in six games. Needless to say, I was in the extreme minority. As stated, this year was the 50th anniversary of the Mets Miracle, when the Amazins upset the heavily favored Baltimore Orioles. That historic accomplishment almost had a repeat in 1973 when the Mets were in the World Series again, de-

CHAPTER 11

spite winning only 83 games, just two games over .500. Zany relief pitcher's Tug McGraw's charge, "Ya Gotta Believe," became the mantra of New York City.

The Darling-Knight-Tina coincidence got me thinking. Minor things, but the timing got me fantasizing. Maybe us all being here in DC was not a coincidence but some kind of family karma. Baseball can be mystical. Then I began analyzing. My conclusion: these were not coincidences; they were signs:

- Nolan Ryan was a rookie member of the '69 Mets and an important part of their winning World Series pitching staff that year. As executive advisor to the (cheating) Astros, Ryan sat conspicuously, on a nightly basis, behind home plate of every Astro playoff and World Series game. You could not miss seeing him on national television.
- Both these Astros and the 1969 Orioles had won the most wins in their franchise history. Both were heavy favorites to win the World Series.
- Davey Johnson, former manager for the Nationals, was the winning manager of the aforementioned (Tina in the Connecticut family room) Championship Mets of 1986. He was also the first playoff manager of the Nationals (see the above 2012 NLDS).
- As a Baltimore Oriole player, this same Johnson made the final out of the 1969 World Series against

the Mets. Thus producing the forever, wonderful Met fan memory of centerfielder Cleon Jones catching the ball then going down on one knee in a genuflection and acceptance of the championship.

Prior to the Series I actually developed an Excel spreadsheet showing that Max Scherzer would be Tom Seaver, Stephen Strasburg would be Jerry Koosman, and maybe Sean Doolittle could be Tug McGraw. Plus, the National hitters would continue to hit those long fly ball outs, except now they will be soaring over the walls in diminutive Minute Maid Park in Houston. People assumed that I was old or nuts or both.

The teams returned to Houston's band box for the final two games. The National pitchers and coaching staff were obviously aware of the Astros' unfair home spying advantage, the infamous sign stealing scheme. The Nats created a complex set and system of pitching signs. The Houston cheaters could not hit because they did not know what pitch was coming.

On the other side of things, the Nationals hitters saw the ball very well. They hit five home runs, amassed 18 hits, and outscored Houston 13–4 in the two games.

In the end my prediction was incorrect, technically. The Nationals were victorious, but it had taken them seven games, not my predicted six.

Tina and Will were finally baseball-happy in Washington. I had personally witnessed another World Se-

CHAPTER 11

ries Championship in my new hometown and a baseball record—the only time in history when the World Series Champions won all four of its victories on the road.

Timing is everything, as seems to be my location

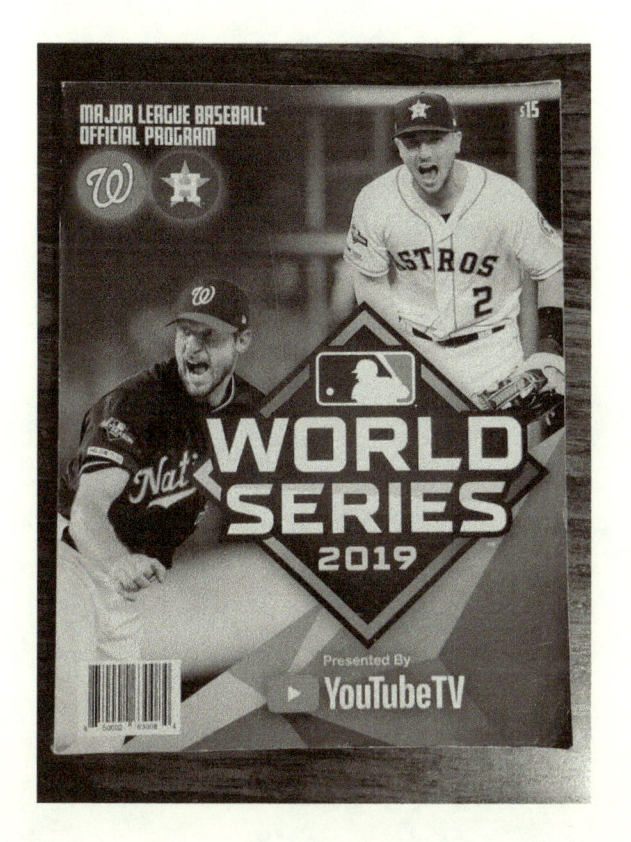

CHAPTER 12

CLUBHOUSE - BORED IN BOSTON

September 2, 2001

Friends and family had just completed three marvelous days packed with activities celebrating the wedding of our first daughter, Cristina. The weekend weather was spectacular. The company was more than enjoyable. Every planned detail was flawlessly executed. The occasional detour was managed with such grace or imagination that it added to the lasting memories. The culminating event was a formal Saturday evening reception at The Inn at Longshore, an establishment nestled on the rocky, sandy shores of Long Island Sound in Connecticut. The six hours of sheer fun ended quite late. It was now the next day. A small gathering of friends together with new and old family had assembled on our backyard deck for a casual Sunday barbecue.

Conversation drifted to baseball, as we were in the dog days of August. George Savage, son-in-law of my Uncle Emil, is a Yankees fan. As a matter of course he brought up the previous World Series, which was of the Subway variety held in New York City. The championship series was the first of the new century, during which his team quickly dispatched of mine in five games.

True Mets fans expect their team to lose. I find this to be almost always the case, at least for the honest and sane. Affinity and attraction lie in the patient wait for the drama to unfold. Victory does not elude the Mets. Rather the riddle is, how are they going to snatch defeat this time? A fatalistic but factual adventure. To err is to be human. We are supposed to make mistakes. Only we can call them our own. Hopefully, we get another chance, or our second wind. The Mets certainly do. For them, the wind is always blowing in. (I reference here a new book authored by Devin Gordon: *So Many Ways to Lose: The Amazin' True Story of the New York Mets – The Best Worst Team in Sports*. One way or the other, it will bring you to tears).

I purposely interrupted this Yankee banter of my baseball friend, George. I mentioned that I had suddenly come into related and recent good fortune. A company vendor had supplied us with four box seat tickets to a clash between archrivals: the Red Sox and the Yankees, in historic Fenway Park. It was just two weeks away, but no one but me had agreed to their assigned seating. I was looking for three other willing occupants.

CHAPTER 12

I made an offer that George could not refuse. I suggested that he and I take my dad and Dad's brother on a road trip to Boston. He was apoplectic.

George is not a Yankees season ticket-holder but probably should be. He attends so many games and has done so for so many years, the Yanks could charge him rent. He has friends in high places—and not just those seated beyond the outfield. It is not clear if he is officially a *Bleacher Creature*. I really did not want to know. George regularly sits behind the mayor's box adjacent to the dugout and nearby the Yankees on-deck circle. The Yankees players may not know his name, but many would recognize him.

He had never been to Fenway in his life—needless to say, nor for a classic rivalry game. He was all in. Now onto the hard part—convincing our elders.

Both Brooklyn-born, John and Emil possessed no keen interest in seeing the Yankees play. This would be the case even if the game were local and played in the Bronx. The idea of two senior citizen, World War II veteran brothers seated together in the rear seat during a three-hour drive to Boston in Labor Day weekend traffic was unappealing, if not downright daunting. George and Emil would even have the additional drive of two hours (without traffic) from South Ozone Park, in Queens, to the proposed launching pad here in Ridgefield.

Since the exodus of the Dodgers, Dad had developed into just a casual baseball fan—though he did keep his eye on the Yanks. Emil, not so much, either before or after Brooklyn's departure. We won over Dad fairly quickly; his brother was an entirely different matter. After two hours of burgers, beers, and private conversation, he eventually acquiesced. (I was not privy to the number of car washings and lawn cuttings committed. That remained entirely a family matter between George and Emil.) The four of us were all set and all in...more or less.

The game happened to be the nationally televised Sunday Night Baseball broadcast on ESPN television—popular, and already ten years old. Part of the draw was the push and pull commentary of its announcers, the entertaining duo of John Miller and Hall of Fame player, Joe Morgan. Their gig lasted for two decades.

I knew the road to Massachusetts well from countless long drives to our bakery customers spread across New England. We needed to find a couple of hotel rooms, which was no small challenge. It was the Sunday of summer's last holiday weekend in Boston. The city was one of the top historic sites in the Northeast and quite a draw for tourists. We accomplished our mission, however. Our reservations took us to a two-star Days Inn in Brighton[1].

---

1   As a strange coincidence, as fate would have it, this became the same hotel where the September 11 terrorists held up, just a few days after our stay, in the week before they hijacked American Airlines Flight # 11 at Logan Airport and flew into the World Trade Center's North Tower (See 7th Inning).

CHAPTER 12

We all survived the drive and found the hotel, after which we found a taxi, Italian sausage and peppers sandwiches on Yawkey Way, and Fenway.

The location of our seats was fantastic, albeit all seats in this stadium seem close to the action and playing field. The smaller capacity and its design create this atmosphere. An original since 1912, the old-style stadium is a cathedral of baseball. But even so, our seats were almost *on* the field. Three rows away from the home plate side of the visitor dugout placed us really, really close. George was nearly close enough to his hero in the on-deck circle (Derek Jeter) to pine tar his bat for him, or certainly to have a conversation (which he did). Leading off, #2, while warming up in the visitor's on-deck circle, he recognized George, smiled, and said, "What are you doing *here*? Nice seats."

The crowd was full capacity, as usual. There was a pregame buzz in the night air, with the end of the summer, prime time television, media trucks, and the kids returning to school. George wore his official Yankees away jersey and was in full Bomber regalia. When nearby fans demanded to know where he got the ticket, he just pointed to me. I sheepishly made no eye contact.

I decided to keep an official tab of the proceedings with my scorecard. It was destined to be a great pitcher's duel. We were sitting right there, up close and personal, near both the pitching mound and home plate. The matchup featured the Moose, Mike Mussina, and David

Cone. Mussina was a future Hall of Famer and Cone was a Cy Young Award winner. In 1999 and on Manager Joe Torre's birthday, Cone had pitched a perfect game in Yankee Stadium, only the third in their history. That was two seasons ago. Now Cone was a Red Sox. This was Mussina's first year with New York. To expect that this game would highlight great pitching did not take baseball genius. These two were quite the pitching pair. Their combined lifetime pitching statistics take your breath away: 6,460 innings, 464 wins and 5,481 strikeouts. Their strikeouts, if counted consecutively, would span more than a full season's worth of batters, over 200, nine-inning games.

I had followed David Cone's career. Cone was a New York Met for the first five full years of his career, including his one and only 20-game-winning season in 1988. The classic power pitcher had now turned to finesse in this, the last full year of his career. On the other side, Mussina would amass 278 career victories and play out his career with the Yanks, retiring in 2008.

The game was moving along very quickly, especially for an American League game with its contrived Designated Hitter (DH) high scoring.

What was interesting to observe, especially with a Mets fan perspective, was the general pessimism of the Red Sox fans and their nagging. They were still under the "Curse of the Bambino" (when Babe Ruth was traded to New York) and still had not won a World Series

CHAPTER 12

Championship since 1918. They would second guess every move of their manager, who was a new one, since they had just fired Jimy Williams a few weeks earlier. Williams had taken the team to the playoffs two of his four years and was voted AL Manager of the year in 1999. The team went downhill after the switch for the rest of this year.

Both pitchers were mowing down their competition, inning after inning. Both were better than good, but Mussina was a tad better. He had struck out five of the first six batters he faced (and Cone was the strikeout pitcher). They matched zeros into the fifth inning, and then again in the sixth. The realization hit me then that the Red Sox had not yet had a single base runner—eighteen batters up, eighteen batters down.

More of the same in the seventh inning. I announced this to the fans seated around us. Most were unaware. Those few with pencils in hand peered over their reading glasses and scorecards, simply nodding back, confirming the accuracy of my statement. The buzz of the crowd returned more loudly to the stadium, especially in between innings.

The mildly interested Emil (he might have nodded off for three or four batters) mentioned that he was at a game just like this once, at Ebbets Field in Brooklyn. The Dodger pitcher was Sal Maglie, who he proudly remembered was known as "the Barber." Apparently, Sal often pitched close inside. I asked him what had happened back then. Emil simply stated, "It was boring. He pitched a no-hitter."

I double checked my scorecard.

The historical record shows that in 1956, Maglie allowed no hits in a complete game, ending in a win against the Philadelphia Phillies. He was not exactly perfect; he issued two walks, and unsurprisingly, hit one batter. So far, Moose had been better.

The pitchers traded goose eggs again in the eighth. Finally, the Yankees broke through against Cone, plating a run in the top of the ninth, aided by a Red Sox ground ball error, which should have been an inning-ending double play.

In the bottom of the inning, the Red Sox's first batter hit a shot which was aiming for the right field corner. The Yankee first baseman made a great play, catching up with it and firing back to the five-time Gold Glove Winner, Mussina, who was covering the bag at first. Thirty-three thousand were on their feet. Two outs to go for a no-no and perfect game.

Mussina then struck out the second batter for his 13th strikeout and 26th consecutive out. Now, one more to go. The Red Sox sent up a pinch-hitter, Carl Everett. Mussina quickly got two strikes, but then missed with a high fast ball. The stadium crowd became noticeably quiet. (Earlier in the year, Mussina faced Everett four times in a game and struck him out all four times.) He now remained just one strike away from that rare, perfect-game pitching performance.

On the next pitch, Everett punched a soft but clean base hit to left center field, the opposite way.

Mussina had missed being perfect by *one* pitch. The Boston fans' immediate reaction was mostly cheers for the historic Yankee moment being spoiled. Then, the crowd did give a standing ovation for the effort. Moose got the final batter to ground out, preserving the shutout and settling for his one-hit gem.

We had witnessed an exciting and classic game (I dislike the word "epic," since everything simply cannot be). The four of us shuffled out of Fenway to the classy chants of "Yankees Suck! Red Sox Suck!" and in search of another cab. George checked Fenway off his bucket list and coveted his ticket stub, possibly as a good omen for the Yankees' season. As it turned out, the Yankees did make it to the World Series (*see 8th Inning*). Mussina won one game, but the Bombers lost to the Diamondbacks in Arizona.

BOSTON RED SOX
VS
New York
Yankees
Sunday
September 2, 2001
TBD Game 68
Game Time 1:05 or 8:05 p.m.
BOSTON RED SOX
1901 2001
FRIENDLY FENWAY
$55.00 A
Account #417479
RAIN CHECK 002001
BOX 54 J 2
SECT BOX ROW SEAT

CHAPTER 13

BENCH - CENTURY'S PRE-GAME

July 13, 1999

In days bygone, companies would run special sales incentive programs to reward peak performers and to create a special focus for a sales organization. Sales contests instilled friendly competition and a focus on important objectives. Rewards ranged in type—clocks, gift cards, barbecue grills, trophies, watches, travel rewards, and incentive trips. Shortly after I joined the family-owned bakery company, I instituted a similar quarterly program, rewarding the best performance four times a year. Winners were regional and scope was national. Fifty were vying for five spots. The theme was sports, as they were generally popular and performance oriented. In *Fast Break*, sales executives competed for a trip to the NCAA (National Collegiate Athletic

Association) *Final Four* weekend of the national basketball championship. *PRO Performance* earned the winner a trip to the PGA's (Professional Golf Association) US Open. The *Winner's Circle,* the Kentucky Derby.

I usually attended and personally entertained the winning group. This was a direct order—one rarely ignored since it came directly from me. This was particularly true of the case in the summer of 1999. I was quicker than ever to oblige this call to duty. After all, it was baseball. The *All-Star* sales contest awarded the top sales producers with a trip to Major League Baseball's All-Star Game.

I did have the good fortune of previously attending one Midsummer Classic. When I was still in the world of Maxwell House, the 1988 version occurred in Cincinnati, contested at Riverfront Stadium. Coffee was my ticket to Ohio. I have a Pete Rose autographed baseball (see *3rd Inning*), which was gifted to me the prior night, to prove it. Rose was one of the key sparkplugs of the Cincinnati Reds *Big Red Machine* which dominated the game in the 70s and is still the best team in baseball history.

About the only thing I recall is that there were more New York Mets than New York Yankees selected. For me this was an enjoyable theme which played out in this decade. The 80s recorded one of the only two Mets World Championships in their sixty years. A Mets fan's chance to crow is minimal and fleeting. This was one of those few times.

CHAPTER 13

Regardless, the 1999 event would be different. The All-Star Game in July was in its 66th year, but not in its 66th game. From 1933 through 1948 they played twice, excluding 1945 due to World War II. There was an East and a West location. I assume this was so that more fans across the country had the opportunity to attend. (Back then, Cincinnati, St. Louis, Chicago, and probably even Detroit were in the "west" for some.)

The contest winners were a motley crew. Our All-Star bakery lineup included a wide-ranging assortment of sales professionals. New England Mike (see *8th Inning*); Windy City Doug—the Scotsman, now likely on a boat in Florida; Twin Cities Tim; Smith from the Canyon State; Hoppe from Cincinnati; Jerry Hill from the Kansas flatlands; Jesse and Lonnie of the Wild West; and last, but certainly not least, Betsy from Corporate. I am somewhat confident that this list is not 100 percent accurate, since we had just five regions. I could be conflating winners of other great venues, Kentucky Derby or Pebble Beach. However, this group seems to make for more interesting writing (and hopefully reading).

This was to be the final All-Star game of the twentieth century and played inside one of baseball's few remaining cathedrals. This supposedly was to be one of the final years of Fenway Park, which opened in Boston in 1912. The Red Sox ownership had announced a great dig and planned construction of a new, downtown, modern stadium (which never happened).

The winners flew into Logan Airport and rallied at our hotel on the Charles River. In the afternoon, some wandered the nooks and bookstores of Cambridge while others sought out the American Revolution. On the first night we had a great dinner at a restaurant which I cannot recall. It could have and should have been Legal Seafood. For sure we ended the evening in Boston's North End. All savored classic Italian desserts at Mike's Pastry. Mike's is but a few steps away from the house of Paul Revere. Price of admission was an obligatory downing of one (the first for all of the winners) shot of grappa—an experience worth watching by this paying author.

After spending the next day relaxing, sight-seeing, or on conference calls with customers, we gathered again. This time it was more official and at Major League Baseball's hotel headquarters. The pregame VIP cocktail reception and banquet included a featured speaker. We enjoyed a talk of funny and entertaining baseball tales by former pitcher, Jim Bouton, the aforementioned author of the sport's most important book, *Ball Four.*

Time heals all wounds, I guess, even for Major League Baseball. When Bouton first published his fascinating social document, he was immediately viewed as a social leper by most sportswriters, stirring up a hornet's nest with the league and many players—and therefore, also with a large segment of fans (I am guessing mostly the older ones). The well-publicized controversy turned out to be an effective and free publicity campaign. The 1970 original printing was five thousand copies. Total sales have reached over 500,000 hardcovers and five million paperbacks since, proving that truth does sell. Now, 30 years later, here he was headlining a pregame event to baseball's marquee game.

A *connection* (New England Mike) reminded me of a Mickey Mantle story shared that evening by Bouton. This lifetime Yankees fan would never forget it. Evidently, I had. The Yankees were playing a day game in the Bronx. Mantle's name was not on perennial Manager Casey Stengel's lineup card. Mickey was still under the influence of the previous late night's escapade. It ended up being a close game, ready to go into extra innings. The Bombers had run out of pinch hitters. The Mick was not on the bench in the Yankees' dugout, but rather in the club house, appropriately laid out on a training table, fast asleep. Stengel (more likely and probably Manager Ralph Houk) awakened him and ordered him to pinch hit. The aging player obliged.

The Kid staggered waywardly into his batter's box. Boy, was this at bat going to be a long shot. That is exactly what it ended up becoming. Mantle hit a walk-off, game-winning homerun. Bouton later asked the veteran hero how he accomplished the feat, considering his condition and all. The hero's response: "I saw three balls coming at me and I hit the one in the middle."

After, we all headed over to Fenway. We fanned our way through the usually colorful Red Sox fans outside on Lansdowne Street, many staggering in from Brookline or Van Ness. Inside, we found our group seats out in the right field upper deck grandstands.

This summer classic had the customary, star-studded lineup, full of future Hall of Famers. This evening in Boston were the Juniors—Cal Ripken and Ken Griffey, Pedro Martinez, Piazza, Randy Johnson, Mariano Rivera, Greg Maddux, and more. Cone and Mussina were even there, but this time as a Yank and an Oriole (See *Clubhouse*). Then there was the other group selected for their power and conditioning (rather conditions)—Mark Maguire, Sammy Sosa, Jose Canseco, Roger Clemens, Manny Ramirez, among others—clearly the favorites of the then MLB Commissioner. What we could not and did not anticipate was the opening ceremony.

For this, Major League Baseball also gets credit, with kudos to its marketing and event planning departments. The pregame activity centered on the winners of the All-Century Team. Two million fans had voted for, selecting from an expertly compiled list, the 100 greatest players of the century. Position by position, spanning all eras and generations of modern times: Ruth, Walter Johnson, DiMaggio, Ty Cobb, Yogi Berra, even the unlisted Pete Rose. In a celebratory yet solemn ceremony, each player appeared out of their respective league dugout and jogged or walked to their on-field playing location - position by position, player by player, the eldest assisted. Every living player named to the team attended. For me and for most everybody else, it was emotional.

Are you kidding me! All these baseball heroes, on the same field at the same moment in time. So many of them I had watched on television when I was a kid or followed at a game or just simply read about on plaques photographed during a lucky visit to Cooperstown, New York: Henry Aaron+, Willie Mays, Stan Musial, Ernie Banks, Warren Spahn, Juan Marichal, Bob Gibson+, Brooks Robinson, Tom Seaver+, Nolan Ryan, Mike Schmidt, and on and on. Four were actually in both events, the pregame ceremony and the night's All-Star Game: Griffey and Ripken, also McGwire and Clemens—the four still active and still popular enough to be an All-Star.

Incredulously to me, two players had missed the voting cut with the fans: Warren Spahn (#10 among pitchers) and Stan Musial (#11 among outfielders), these two from my childhood watching era. Spahn is the winningest lefty of all time (363 Wins). Musial accomplished a lifetime batting average of .331 and was 24 hits short of having 1000 more than Ted Williams (and where was Teddy, anyway?). Good God! Between the two, Musial and Spahn combined for 41 years of All-Star game appearances. They had played the bulk of their careers without the benefit of nationally televised games and partly before World War II. Thankfully, a select panel later added the two into the all-century roster, along with three others.

Sandy Koufax, an All-Century selection himself (#2), was asked which player was the greatest left-handed pitcher in history: himself (with three times as many votes) or Spahn. Koufax picked Spahn, saying, "Not only for what he did on the field; he pitched in the whole damn century."

A digression is required here.

Spahn of the Braves and Marichal of the Giants—it is always special when a HOF pitching matchup is scheduled—when the players are still playing and not yet in the HOF. These two squared off in Candlestick Park in San Francisco on one summer day. Incredibly, each pitched a complete game of *16 innings* (15 1/3 for Spahn). Warren gave up a walk-off home run to baseball's greatest player, Willie Mays, in arguably the greatest game ever pitched. The Milwaukee Braves lost 1–0. The two aces faced a combined total of 115 batters, hurling a total of 488 pitches (227/Marichal, 261/Spahn) in a game that lasted only four hours and 10 minutes. That's more than three games for the modern game's pitcher, considering controlled pitch counts and situational specialists. What a difference 60 years make. If there was ever a case for not leaving a great game before it has ended it is this epic marathon of July 2, 1963. *The Greatest Game Ever Pitched,* authored by Jim Kaplan, allows you to relive it inning by inning, via dual biographies.

If all that history and pageantry were not enough, no one could ever forget the ceremonial first pitch and the answer to the crowd's question of "where the hell is Teddy Baseball?"

Boston's own Ted Williams, via golf cart, was escorted from the Red Sox bullpen. A waving Williams, a frenzied Fenway. The Splendid Splinter came in to repeat his ceremonial first throw of 1961, in the first year of his retirement and the last time this park hosted the game. All the current game's All-Stars gathered around him, his cart, and driver on the pitcher's mound, jockeying to get closer—a friendly but moblike scene. FOX TV stayed on the air for over 38 consecutive minutes, without commercial break, to witness the spectacle.

There was a game after all this. Most will not remember much of it, probably with one notable exception: its first two innings. Hometown favorite and pitching great, Red Sox Pedro Martinez, struck out five of the first six batters which he faced. Delirium arrived again in Fenway, K by K. He became the first pitcher to strike out the side to begin an All-Star Game, for which Pedro earned the game's MVP Award.

If the fans voted today, Martinez would have made the "greatest pitcher" list. In fact, at his best, he may have been the best pitcher ever. In the book *The Baseball 100*,

Joe Posnanski points out: "Now look at him through the Baseball-Reference prism. Baseball reference evaluates pitchers based on how many runs they allow, the ballpark where they play, and how good the defense is behind them. By those measures, Martinez's 2000 season has an argument as the greatest ever. That year, he had a 1.74 ERA (when the league-wide ERA was 4.92), struck out 284 in 217 innings, and walked 32, even fewer than he had in 1999. His ERA+ of 291 that year was the highest in modern baseball history by a long shot."

For the record, the final: American League 4, National League 1.

Credit is due where credit is due. Bud Selig, Milwaukee's beer magnate, was professional baseball's Steroid Comish. Some All-Star players were packed with so many performance enhancing drugs (PEDs) that you could not tell who was bigger than whom, even with binoculars. Check out YouTube to see for yourself—Sosa, Maguire, Ramirez, Clemens. Unlike so many on the field that evening, none of these were enshrined in Cooperstown, and they will possibly be kept out forever.

I was more than "lucky" to be at this historic event, but I was even more fortunate three days later to be off to Greece and Turkey on our 25th wedding anniversary trip.

+ As this writing has struggled through its passage, these greats, nominated or selected on this evening, have passed on. The timing is unfathomable, at least

CHAPTER 13

for an aging author:

Frank Robinson	02/07/19
Al Kaline	04/06/20
Tom Seaver	08/31/20
Lou Brock	09/06/20
Bob Gibson	10/02/20
Joe Morgan	10/11/20
Henry Aaron	01/22/21

CHAPTER 14

BULLPEN - PERFECT PERCH

July 27, 2017

This was our first summer of residence in Washington, DC. This provided me with the opportunity to plan individual trips with each of my three grandchildren. Today was the middle one's turn.

Six-year-old Wynn played both organized soccer and Little League baseball on Capitol Hill. He had already made the travel soccer club. This was his first year in Little League. Sagely, Wynn already knew that his favorite game to play was soccer, but that his favorite sport to watch was baseball. Therefore, I was not surprised with his response when I questioned him about what he wanted to do on his special day with Papo. Wynn regularly attended Washington Nationals games, as he practically had since infancy. I was somewhat confused with the details of his response. The conversation went something like this:

P "So, Wynn, what do you want to do?"

W "Go to a ball game and see the Nationals."

P "OK, what else?"

W "Can we sit somewhere different this time?"

P "Sure...what do you mean?"

W "Papo, our seats are always too close to the field."

P "Well yes, they usually are. Maybe you would like to sit out in the outfield this time?"

W "Yes, that's what I mean."

P "How about behind your favorite player, Bryce Harper,* in right or center field?"

W "Yes, that would be good. I would like that."

* At that time, Harper, an original National, was a young phenom; at the time of this writing, he has since moved on to a new lucrative contract with division ri-

CHAPTER 14

vals, the Philadelphia Phillies, where he was the National League's MVP in 2021. He is no longer fancied by Wynn, who discarded and recycled his Harper bobblehead.

I dutifully procured two tickets. The seats were located in the first row of the lower deck in right center field, above the out-of-town scoreboard, which we could not see. We certainly *could* see the sun, as we would for the entire game. Shining brightly down upon us, the temperature had already climbed to eighty-two degrees at first pitch; a slight was breeze out, but temperatures were on the rise—unfriendly to pitching. Hot and not covered, we did have Bryce's back.

12:05 was an unusually early start for a day game. A large crowd was pouring into the ballpark—over 33,000, uncommon for a weekday afternoon. It was Camp Day. Welcoming ushers organized hundreds of young campers by the busload.

Today's opposition was the Milwaukee Brewers, and this was the rubber game of a three-game series on the Thursday getaway, travel day. The Brew Crew would be off to Chicago next to play the Cubs (who, in this season, will outlast them and claim the Central Division title. In late October, those same Cubs would make a visit to DC and quash the World Series aspirations of these same Nationals).

Today's pitcher, Michael Blazek, was making his very first start, but not his major league debut. He had already appeared in games as a relief pitcher, four times, all earlier in this month. Starting for the Nationals was staff ace, Max Scherzer.

The game started typically for the home team. The Nationals jumped ahead, right away, 2–0, in the opening inning. Harper hit a two-run homer in his first at bat. As the ball soared over us, I did notice that Wynn was smiling. The game had started off as planned. Typical, because Washington had no problem scoring runs all season long.

The Nationals would end up leading all National League teams in just two hitting categories this season, slugging percentage (.449) and total bases (2,495). Little did we know how relevant these two specific statistics would be on this Thursday in July.

This game was going to become anything but typical. I should have packed Wynn's batting helmet - as a child safety precaution measure.

The bottom of the third inning started off inauspiciously, yet ominously. The last place hitting Scherzer drew a walk, a gift delivered by Blazek. Today was Mad Max's birthday. It is never a clever idea to walk the opposing pitcher to lead off an inning. The next batter was leadoff hitter Brian Goodwin who promptly smacked a deep two-run home run, which also sailed right over our heads. Then the very next batter, Wilmer Difo, repeated, crushing a deep shot into the upper deck in right field, over our heads once again, only higher. Back-to-back, and pretty cool. That does not happen

CHAPTER 14

every day. Wynn's smile was growing.

His turn now—the aforementioned Harper joined the parade, launching his second home run of the game, this time to our right, deep into the centerfield stands. Three in a row! I exclaimed, "Holy Cow!" and explained to this now wide-eyed Little Leaguer what a religious farm animal had to do with a homer. It was an exclamation popularized by Yankee Phil Rizzuto for 40 years in the Bronx. (The Scooter began his broadcasting career in the 50s when Papo was his grandson's age).

"Geez Louise!" (courtesy again of Rizzuto, probably also Harry Carey). At this point, what was the pitcher Blazek thinking? Maybe, *Please Coach, come and get me! Get out of that dugout and please put me in it, PLEASE*?

Original Washington franchise player, Ryan Zimmerman, was next up in the batting order to face Blazek. The third baseman had delivered historically before, christening this new park on its opening day by slamming a walk off homerun in the bottom of the ninth inning for its nascent victory. Guess what happened next? Zim homered again, this time hitting a rocket, a liner over the fence into the visitor's bullpen.

Back-to-back-to-back-to-back! Only eight teams in baseball history had hit four consecutive homers. The Nationals became the first club to accomplish it with their number one-through-four hitters. What about #5? Now anything seemed possible. They did have the right player coming up.

Daniel Murphy was the author's recent (former) hero, Most Valuable Player of the New York Mets Championship run in 2015. The second baseman accomplished this by impersonating Babe Ruth for two weeks in Los Angeles, Chicago, and New York. Murphy hit so many home runs (seven) that he broke playoff records. Unfortunately for the Mets, the opposition figured that out in the World Series, when he ceased and desisted.

Murph did connect for a fly ball, but this one decided to stay inside the park, being shallow, landing in the rightfielder's mitt right in front of us. With a smile he returned to the dugout to the mock boos of a spoiled crowd and raucous young campers. This provided everyone with a chance to catch a breath and return to their seat. They had been standing and screaming for a long while now, and they were finally getting a minute to talk about what had just happened.

Except for the very next batter. Anthony Rendón hit a home run deep to left centerfield. Hitting five home runs in six at bats in the same inning tied another major league record.

The Brewers mercifully changed pitchers. Blazek belatedly headed to the showers or directly to the airport, or to whereabouts unknown. A good guess would be to all three. The Nationals scored one more time in this same inning. This one did not come by way of another four-bagger, just a loud double, unbelievably still with just one out. After another hit, this one by the

CHAPTER 14

birthday boy pitcher, the barrage finally ended. Goodwin, the Nat who started everything in the first place in this historical inning, sharply lined into the hole at short. The third baseman made a great play, spearing it and turning it into a double play and catching Max off the bag at first.

Line score for this inning: 7 runs, 8 hits, 0 errors, 1 left on base.

The Nationals hit two more home runs in the next inning, Zimmerman adding his second of the game. The game's eight home runs established a new franchise record. When completed, this one ended 15–2, more of a football score than baseball. Washington had recorded 19 hits and 48 total bases.

Quite amazingly, the Brewer starter became the first—and he remains, today, the only—pitcher in Major League history to allow five home runs in the same inning (it's possible that this "feat" may have been matched recently, here in 2022). Blazek only pitched in five games for Milwaukee. This was his last. He was out of the big leagues for the next two years, though curiously, he did play in one more season in 2019. Curious because it was for just four games, all in the month of July, and for the Washington Nationals.

As we rose from our outfield seats to commence our walk home, I looked over to my grandson, saying: "You were right. We always do sit too close." Once again Wynn smiled.

1	2	3	4	5	6	7	8	9	R	H	E
0	0	0	1	0	0	1	0	0	2	4	1
2	0	7	6	0	0	0	-	-	15	19	0

CHAPTER 15

THE SHOWERS - FATHER'S DAY "GIFT"

July 31, 2018

2018 marked my second Father's Day in the nation's Capital, having relocated a year earlier. Daughter #1, Cristina—at one time a Mets fan, but now one of the Nationals—gifted me (really us) a baseball game for the occasion: Washington Nationals versus the New York Mets at Nationals Park. It was to be a part of the ongoing interdivisional and intrafamily rivalry.

She decided to splurge this time: two club-level seats had been procured, and were located just five rows behind home plate. This location is one where you will eat and drink all you want without necessarily getting off your bottom or out of your seat.

As usual, both teams were competitive—in this particular season, more with each other than the rest of the league. With over 100 games in the books, the Nats were a .500 team, 53–53. The Mets were 16 games short of that. This may turn out to be one of those rare years when neither club makes the playoffs (neither team did—the Mets ended the year with 77 wins and the Nationals with 82).

Unfortunately, when Game Day arrived, Daughter #1 was ill and called in sick, placed on the family's IL (Injured List). I penciled Granddaughter #1, Carmen, into the attending lineup. (It did not dawn on me at the time, and actually not until now, that today was the birthday of my mother-in-law, Carmen, who would have been the great-grandmother to my new sidekick, her namesake.)

Great summer weather welcomed us on this last evening of July. Carmen had been attending Nat games for over a decade, despite only being ten years old. She has enjoyed lemonade, cotton candy, cracker jacks, and peanuts in this ballpark all her life.

I thought that this would be a wonderful opportunity to teach her how to keep score of the ballgame. This would also not hurt the development of her observational and mathematical skills. Our first stadium purchase included two hot dogs, a lemonade, a lager, a pencil, and a scorecard.

Today's Mets starter was a promising, young left-hander who hailed from Long Island, Steven Matz. Tanner Roark, himself an up-and-coming youngster, was the starting pitcher for the Nationals.

CHAPTER 15

In addition to enjoying supper, our pregame activities included filling out the player lineups, recording the batting order, and explaining the numerical coding system for their corresponding fielding positions. A battery of example plays was sample scored. The fundamental symbols—strikeouts, walks, errors, fly balls, and ground outs—were all reviewed.

Carmen seemed to understand, but did seem somewhat dazed. There would be plenty of time for on-the-job training after the delivery of the first pitch. There were endless scenarios to consider and log—pinch hitters, new pitchers, long innings with multiple at bats, pitch counts. I dispensed with the rest at this early point in the evening. This preserved the sanity of the young student, but tested the resolve of the old teacher.

A natural rivalry had developed between these two teams in the National League's East Division, despite the Mets being 56 years old and the Nationals just 12. The 2016 signing of one Daniel Murphy strengthened the conflict. Formerly a NY Met, Daniel is today a living and walking example of Murphy's Law (if anything can go wrong, it will). The three-year contract immediately followed the Mets' run into the 2015 World Series. Murphy was on a home run tear and was a critical cog in how and why the Mets bushwhacked the Chicago Cubs and then took care of the Los Angeles Dodgers in the two National League playoff rounds. New York opted not to re-sign him to a new deal. The Nationals did.

In his first two years as a National, Murph became a two-time All-Star, finished second in the 2016 Most Valuable Player voting, led the league in doubles, and compiled season batting averages of .347 and .322. In 2016, he led the league in slugging percentage (.595) and on-base percentage (.985), playing in over 140 games each year. The Nationals won the division in 2015 and 2016—in both years. He even brought the former Mets hitting coach with him to Washington. I am no expert at baseball analytics or the new sabermetrics, *Moneyball* and all, but clearly those results delivered a high return on investment.

Time flies by. Matz had been with the Mets for four years already. (This may be only to me, but I think he resembles a young Joe DiMaggio, facially.) I recall watching his first game played at Citi Field in 2015. In his Major League pitching debut, which he won 7–2, he came within one out of completing a full eight innings.

Better than that, Matz was better at the plate, amazingly going three for three and driving in four of the seven Mets runs. Steven finished the year with a win-loss record of 4–0, started two postseason playoff games, and even started Game #4 of the World Series, on Halloween no less. What a dream come true for a kid who played his high school baseball just 50 miles away. Matz had not even played enough games that year to qualify as his rookie season, and there he was, starting and pitching in three postseason games. It

CHAPTER 15

happens—but not that often, and even less for a locally grown player who grew up a Mets fan. (Although I just remembered LA Dodger Larry Sherry in 1959.)

Boy, what a difference a day makes.

The Mets opened up the game with a leadoff single which was immediately erased, the runner thrown out at second base. We did not use our eraser. There was nothing much else to report on our scorecard; the Mets held scoreless.

The Nationals opened their first inning the same way, their leadoff hitter getting on board via a ground single. There was a difference: fleet-of-foot Trea Turner promptly stole second. Then he stole third. When Matz struck out the dangerous Anthony Rendón, it looked as though the pitcher might have a chance to get out the inning without too much damage, maybe even without allowing a run. Turned out that those glasses were not to be rose colored, but would be seeing Nationals red.

What ensued and how this game quickly unfolded reminded me of a cartoon: *Baseball Bugs.* Via vintage animation, Bugs Bunny is following the progress of a game from his rabbit hole outside the baseball stadium. The Gas House Gorillas were bludgeoning the outmatched and elderly Teetotalers. The rabbit could not stand it any longer and challenged the gang. Fielding all nine positions, the heroic hare engineered a dramatic come-from-way-behind victory, catching the game-ending long fly ball over six miles away, atop the

"Umpire State Building." The game was set in a stadium resembling the Polo Grounds in upper Manhattan, but with a right field façade similar to that of Yankee Stadium in the Bronx. Since television was in its infancy in 1946, few might have noticed—purposeful and artistic license at it best. In case you missed it, the final score on this one: Bugs 96 Gorillas 95.

Again, I digress—this time, purposely. Speaking of bludgeoning, let us return to my memory and our scorecard. With one out and Turner now on the bag at third, Matz prepared to face the heart of the order. Harper—Zimmerman—Juan Soto—Murphy. This heart showed no love for the Mets pitcher. Double—single—single—single. New score: 3–0.

Then another called strikeout, two outs, with now another chance to limit the damage. This is the National League with no Designated Hitter (DH), yet, so classic strategy was employed: intentionally walk the #8 hitter, load the bases to create the force out at any base, and face the weakest hitting link in the lineup: the pitcher, today, the aforementioned Tanner Roark. Except it did not work. Roark doubled and cleared the bases. New score: 6–0. Ardent baseball fans should lament the day of the installation of the universal DH in the NL. This is just one example of why it will suck; Matz's unexpected hitting prowess in his New York pitching debut is exhibit #2.

Turner and Rendon return to bat again in this, still the first, inning—two more hits. New score: 7–0 . Matz

CHAPTER 15

is finally relieved, but not really. Relief pitcher enters to get the final out. After just one inning, our scorecard is already a mess: 7 runs, 8 hits, 0 errors, 2 LOB. Little did we know that this one inning was merely a sign of things to come.

In the Nationals' second inning, three more runs were highlighted by, of course, a Daniel Murphy two-run home run. New score: 10–0. Well, it probably could not get any worse

Except that it did, in the bottom of the third. Three more runs, all via another home run by Murphy. Have I mentioned Babe Ruth yet? New score: 13–0. Onto the fourth, three more? Yep. This time including another homer, and this one a two-run dinger from Zim. New score: 16–0.

Carmen looked up at me, and then down to the scorecard, and then up at me again. I said we should stay the course and find a new pencil.

Now the fifth inning—with three more runs. Rendón contributed with a bases-loaded triple. New score: 19–0. At this point, the concession crew in our section were mercilessly and graciously serving beer, free to anyone dressed in blue and orange. I obliged. Two scoreless innings for the Nationals and a Mets home run. Could a Mets comeback be brewing?

On to the last at bat by the home team in the eighth. By now, the Mets had expended six pitchers. Enter shortstop, Jose Reyes, to pitch for the first and last time in his big-league career. Instinctively and without delay, I made the decision to tear up the scorecard. Carmen did not understand. I explained to her that sometimes you just have to watch. Besides, her team was crushing mine. Enjoy it.

Reyes had a great Mets career—he had left the team, then returned, and was now in his final playing year. Reyes is the Mets' only batting champion (.337 in 2011); he accumulated over 2,000 career base hits and led the league in stolen bases for three consecutive years (2005–2007). He was an exciting player to watch...when he was hitting.

His pitching debut started off with a deep high fly ball. It went quickly downhill from there. Single, doubles, triple, walks, HPB (hit by pitched ball), home runs. With the Nationals' bench nearly empty via substitutions, they sent up to bat probably their last available position player to pinch hit: Mark Reynolds. As he approached home plate, I predicted a home run—which was not much of a long shot guess. The game had established a clear trend. Reynolds blasted a three-run homer to deep centerfield. With the massacre finally complete, add six more runs. New score: 25–1. Jose Reyes goes into the record books with a lifetime ERA of 54.00.

Despite New York mounting a three-run rally in the top of the ninth, Washington managed somehow to hold on and was victorious. Final score: 25–4.

CHAPTER 15

As we departed the scene of many crimes, I was sure to mention two points to Carmen: firstly, she should thank her mother for my Father's Day *"gift"*; secondly, we needed to try scoring a game again another time.

This time, Carmen understood.

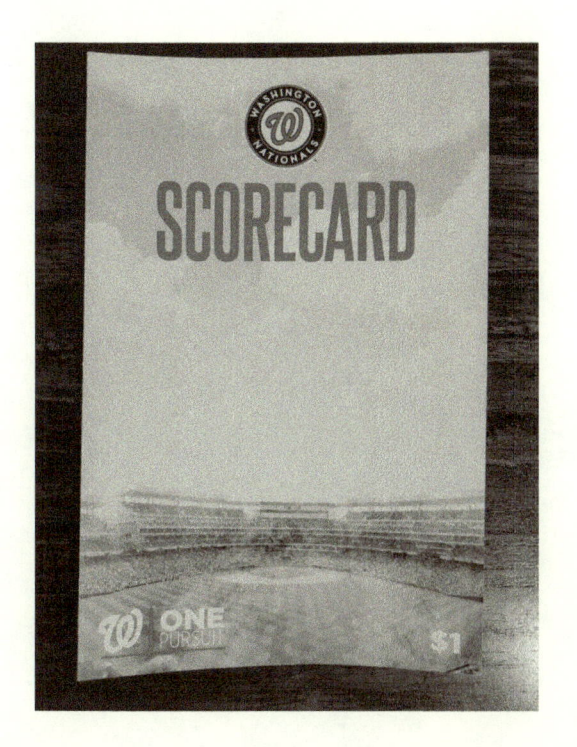

CHAPTER 16

GRANDSTANDS - BASEBALL BOGO

October 24, 2000 - October 30, 2015

If the reader has not been skimming nor has short term memory loss, they would recall that I am a die-hard New York Metropolitan (NY Mets) fan. I apologize if this may seem repetitive—it is partially psychotherapy. This job of being a Mets fan—and it is like a job—is not easy.

Like all franchises, through the years and decades, come the ups and the downs (unless you are a Yankees fan). Over the long term there are excruciating near wins, paltry playoff participation, thrilling losses—but hopefully also a few precious moments.

The Miracle Year—the year in which the New York Mets stunned baseball—was special. It was much more than a moment; it developed into a whole season, capped off with a universally unforeseen World Series victory. For anyone who followed, it really was not a miracle—just wonderful pitching, strong defense, and good hitting. The 1969 World Championship is one of the few precious moments that can be counted, literally, on one Mets fan's hand.

In my first year in college, the Mets plowed through Hank Aaron's Atlanta Braves in Major League Baseball's first Division Series. Under the calm command of former Brooklyn Dodger and now the then Mets manager, Gil Hodges, and guided by a coaching staff composed up of former Dodgers and Yankees catchers (including Yogi Berra), the unlikeliest team rendered the powerful Baltimore Orioles of the American League powerless at the plate.

Hall of Fame Manager Earl Weaver led the O's, which included three fellow Hall of Famers: Brooks and Frank Robinson, as well as ace pitcher Jim Palmer. The Mets dominated Baltimore via their own terrific pitching, behind Tom Terrific (Seaver), Jerry Koosman, Nolan Ryan, Gary Gentry, and a staff of veterans. The lineup rewarded the pitching staff with timely hitting, unlikely power, and spectacular fielding, especially by former American League Rookie of the Year (just three years prior), Tommie Agee. This was as much of a team effort as you could witness.

Since then, World Series appearances have been terrifically thin—only four more times in over 60 years. A longtime New York sports talk radio host would often describe the playoffs as "serious October baseball," marked "serious" since the goal was the World Series. The Mets seriously avoided the series, mostly through poor seasons. A few times when they did come close, they were spoiled.

There was a quick follow-up to the Miracle with a World Series appearance in 1973 with most of the same great pitchers. Yogi Berra now was the manager. Yogi took over the reins after the sudden passing of a very young Gil Hodges (47). (MLB will install Hodges into its Hall of Fame in the year 2022, in which I continue to write). Their opponent was the Oakland Athletics. The A's were a talented team, complete with colorful personalities. Their roster included a Catfish, the Reggie, Fingers, a Blue Moon, Bando, Vida Blue, and even a Jesus. The Mets played them closely. Of course there was a controversial managerial strategic decision (typical Mets drama), but the writing was on the wall—and on the lineup card. In the end, they lost to Oakland, 4–3 games.

Then we waited until 1986 (recall Tina in the Connecticut family room). The Mets had a spectacular team, chock-full of superstars and name brands. The Mets survived a nearly all-day, 21-inning game in Houston earning the right to play the favored Boston Red Sox. This World Series was certainly a moment for both teams and, for their fans, an eternity. As previously mentioned in this book (and now as psychotherapy), a routine grounder, which would have ended the World Series in defeat, found its way through the legs of the Bosox's first baseman. Boston did not shed the curse of the Bambino, and the Mets became World Champions on the next day. The Bad Boys had won. (Thank you for reading this twice)

The talent on this New York Met team was so great that it should have returned to the World Series often. It did not. It was the 80s. Grown men played hard, especially when they were not playing baseball. The Bad Boys were bad. The team underperformed. The Mets never returned to the World Series in the 20th century.

Also, in the 80s, a new retail merchandising concept was emerging. The best that I can tell is that a shoe store chain was the first to concoct the promotion, "Buy One, Get One Free." I recall while in Detroit (*5th Inning*), we developed creative promotions—buy a can of Maxwell House, get a five-pound bag of sugar free. I can still see the ad. Today, BOGO is vernacular within the English language.

Which leads me to this new point. The new century did bring new hope for Mets fans. Along with it came three new eras. The first was with Mike Piazza (*7th Inning*). The second was with the young and exciting infield duo of Jose Reyes (*The Showers*) and David Wright, the former the holder of the team's only batting title and the latter the captain—an exciting tandem, but never in a World Series. They did have 2006, when the

CHAPTER 16

team was "this close." The St. Louis Cardinals hijacked the last playoff game at Shea Stadium—we fans were forever gifted with the vision of Carlos Beltran, his bat lying still on his shoulder, being called out on strikes to end the game (this the same Carlos who hatched the Houston Astros cheating scandal a decade later). The Dark Knight and Thor led the third generation. This pitching duo of Matt Harvey and Noah Syndergaard took New York City by storm.

In 1999, under the managerial leadership of Bobby Valentine, the Mets were "this close" to getting back into the big dance, but were denied by a walk-off walk, the details of which the author will not rehash here a second time (psychotherapy). However, this same Mets club did make a quick encore in the following year, and they did make it to the World Series. The Mets drew the Yankees, who were recent champions and favored in 2000. Las Vegas was correct. The Mets lost, 4–1.

Fast forward fifteen years into a new stadium. Say "Shea" no longer. The Brooklyn-rooted ownership constructed Citi Field in the image and likeness of Ebbets Field, the lost home of the lost Dodgers. This time, in the World Series for the fifth time (most for an expansion team), the Mets drew Kansas City as an opponent. The Royals had homefield advantage because of a dumb All-Star Game rule, since eliminated. KC was waiting longer than the Mets for their next championship. The Mets had been waiting for thirty years; KC, one year longer (1985). The Royals also had lost the previous year's World Series to the SF Giants. They were ready this time. Again, the Mets lose, again, 4–1.

The math is as simple as it can be. In the 21st century (so far), the Mets have won a grand total of two World Series games.

BENNY WITH JOE

In 2000, we all survived the impending catastrophic scare of Y2K. The Mets more than survived the playoffs, plowing through the San Francisco Giants and St. Louis Cardinals to achieve their World Series berth. Many of the wins were exciting, extra-inning and walk-off type victories.

Similar to the golden era, this series was 100 percent New York. This was the first Subway Series since 1956, the first one since the Dodgers and Giants departed west. The opponent Yankees were dominant. The Yanks had rocked baseball to sleep with the snore of their "core four" mini dynasty. The Bombers had won three of the previous four world championships.

This series was a weird one, including a juiced-up Roger Clemens throwing a splintered bat at the head of Piazza in one of the games in the Bronx (after already having beaned him in the helmet during a regular season game). The games were all too painful to witness, or certainly to review. Three of the four losses were by the margin of one run.

CHAPTER 16

I was at the bakery company. My partner in crime was our CFO—better yet, a Mets fan. Joe Talmage caught a pair of tickets from our accounting firm for Game #3. This was the first World Series game in Shea Stadium since the Boys were Bad in 1986. For sure, these seats were not luxury box—we were located in the right outfield, upper grandstands. (As I visualize it now, they were situated weirdly close to my eyewitness seat to Pete Rose's record-breaking hit in the *3rd Inning*). Despite losing the first two games in the Bronx, Shea was still rocking and swaying, literally.

Starting pitching was not exactly a youth drive. The Yanks started "El Duque," Orlando Hernandez; the Mets started Ron Reed. Both were at or close to 35 years of age. Experience counts. There were strikeouts galore. Joe and I were catching an autumn cold from the breeze of all the swinging and missing. (There were a total of 25 strikeouts in the game). Hernandez struck out six of the first seven Mets he faced. His only issue was that the one he missed, did not—Robin Ventura led off the second inning with a home run, putting the Mets faithful into a frenzy. Expectedly, the Yanks fought back and took a 2–1 lead into the bottom of the sixth inning. The Mets tied it up, the run produced by two doubles courtesy of the bats of Piazza and Todd Zeile. Lots of cheering and screaming at Shea!

Then the eighth inning: enter Benny Agbayani. Benny was a newly appointed Mets cult hero. Agbayani was born in Hawaii and selected in the 30th round of the 1993 draft. In the NLCS, he had collected three RBIs helping to defeat the Cardinals. But he truly entered Met infamy with his winning, walk-off home run in the 13th inning here at Shea Stadium against the Giants in Game 3 of their playoff.

Now Zeile had reached base again, this time on a ground ball single. Benny had another moment coming: clubbing a double to deep left centerfield, scoring Todd all the way from first base. Pandemonium in Queens! The Mets then added an insurance run and hung on to beat the Yankees 4–2. To this day, Joe swears it was the best game he has ever witnessed in his life, one in which he lost his voice and, maybe, his souvenir ticket stub.

THOR WITH FRAN

That Dark Knight and his sidekick, Thor, led the Mets into the World Series in 2015. The July trade deadline signing of Yoenis Cespedes was the turning point and the start of a magical ride. The Cuban-born centerfielder lifted the team on his shoulders the rest of the way - amassing 66 hits and 44 RBIs in 57 games. As previously mentioned, (psychotherapy) Daniel Murphy then became Babe Ruth, setting playoff home run records, especially against the Chicago Cubs, who were supposed to win. The Cubs also had a curse of their own, one of seventy years—the curse of the Billie Goat. (In the Mets' first championship season in 1969, a black cat crossed the field in a September regular season game between the two teams. After that day, the Cubs collapsed and the Mets won the division, their first step in that improbable championship journey).

The Mets then powered their way through the Los Angeles Dodgers in the NLCS, winning 3–2 games. I attended one of those victories. Watching Cespedes in Game 3 circling the bases after slamming a monstrous three-run home run to the ending music of the movie *The Natural* is not a visual memory easily forgotten.

My younger sister, Fran, is also a Mets fan. She has two children. The boy, like his father, is a Yankees fan. The girl is not. October 2000 was not fun for the women in the household—but this was now 2015. There were no Yankees in sight. Game #3 of the World Series was the first one in the new Citi Field. It did not matter that the Mets were already trailing the Royals by those two games lost in KC (similar to 2000). We had to be there.

It was cold, football weather. Tomorrow was Halloween and the next day was November. The wind was not gentle but whipping around, especially in the high sections. Thor was the Met starting pitcher. The Royals had been crowding the plate in the first two games, and benefiting. Syndergaard was planning to send a message. He buzzed the leadoff hitter with his first pitch of the game, sending the batter sprawling on his bottom. The Royals took great offense. Mets fans took great delight. It certainly set a new tone. Now in New York City, the crowd was already bananas. The leadoff hitter struck out—more bananas. Regardless, the Royals took a 1–0 lead.

In the bottom of the inning, leadoff hitter Curtis Granderson, Grandy, produced a single. The next batter was David Wright, the aging captain. Wright had endured numerous surgeries, rehabilitation, and physical therapy, eventually enduring career-ending spinal stenosis as well. He had only played in 38 games in the regular season, but he had a bat in his hand in the World Series in Citi Field. The seven-time All Star lifted a fly ball to left centerfield that cleared the wall, a two-run homerun. Billy Joel singing the National Anthem was his lucky charm, I guess.

The Royals stormed right back to take the lead back with their two runs in the next inning, 3–2. Met pitcher Thor led off the following inning with a line drive single. The productive Grandy produced again, hitting a line drive home run, another two runs, another new Mets lead. Bananas Republic!

A Mets four-run outburst in the sixth inning, including two more RBIs from Wright, was icing on the cake—or, rather, Bananas Foster. Mets win, 9–3!

As noted, the Mets' World Series math in the new century is as simple as it can get: two game victories.

CHAPTER 16

The author was lucky enough to witness both, conjuring up an idea for a new retail promotion.

B0G2 (buy none, get two free).

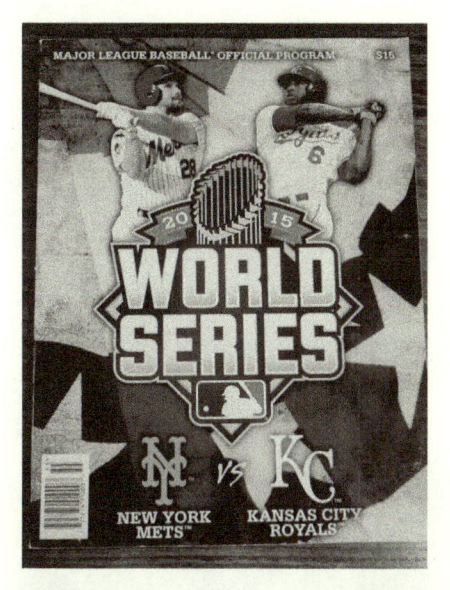

AFTER-FORWARD

I know. I am not sure if that's really a word either. But it is how I feel. I just don't think that I'm done. I know that I have a few more great games left to see. Why not? The airlines are flying again.

When I first set out on writing this book, I was looking forward to this last section—its end. That is no longer the case. I could have rediscovered and reported on another nine or 16 or 32 more games with the aid of their connections, my memories, and research.

Professional advice was that a book should have a conclusion. I will follow that counsel now. In summary:

- Baseball is a great game with unmatched history and drama.
- The sport sparks special memories, earmarking time and space.
- I have been lucky to witness a few of its best games.

Mission accomplished. Epilogue officially recorded.

One quintessential, baseball-summer afternoon, I contemplated what to write here on my regular walk to Eastern Market on Capitol Hill. Like baseball used to be in Brooklyn, this public market is the center of the community and neighborhood, housing purveyors of local fresh foods—butchers, bakers, and candlestick makers (the last on Saturday flea market day). This trek is 25 percent of the way to my other regular walking destination: Nationals Park, Washington's baseball stadium.

This stroll, much like this book, began with the pandemic. For me, the supermarket has transformed into a convenience stop. The market is now my shopping destination. I discovered that the food here is fresher, better, and cheaper. This particular site of Eastern Market opened for business (1873) just about when Major League Baseball (1876) did in Cincinnati.

Washington DC is an international city, which is one reason you may notice more than just Washington National caps in the area. I gain usual comfort running into a NY Met hat and striking up a friendly conversation with a complete stranger.

Baseball does that to people.

As I ordered my tuna at the seafood counter, I did not readily recognize the young man selecting my filet, who was about 25 years young. I did notice his shirt, though. I asked him what was up with the Dodger #22 Kershaw jersey. He announced that LA was his favorite team. I asked him if he knew who the Dodgers' all-time-best left-handed pitcher was. He promptly answered: Koufax. I mentioned that my mom and dad were from Brooklyn, to which he understandingly responded with a smile and thumbs up. As he handed back my credit card, he proudly stated that he had named his new, firstborn child Clayton (as in Kershaw).

Despite the obituaries, baseball does have a future.

(Koufax, Kershaw – baseball does have to fix the demise of the starter.)

On to some of those missing chapters about other great games I have attended and accounted for here:

OPENING DAYS

1976 Yankee Stadium: Bicentennial Year and league championship year

1980 Royals Stadium: league championship year

1984 Tiger Stadium: World Series championship year

2017, 2018, 2019, 2022 Nationals Park: always against the NY Mets, who always win (at least this first game); World Series championship year (2019)

LEAGUE CHAMPIONSHIPS

1980 Royals Stadium: Games #3 and #4 (wins)

1987 Busch Stadium: St Louis Cardinals clinch, Game #7

1989 Wrigley Field: Chicago Cubs lose Game #1 (as usual)

1999 The Ballpark in Arlington (not in Virginia): Game #3, Texas Rangers swept by Yanks

2015 Citi Field: Game #3, Mets beat Dodgers

2019 Nationals Park: Game #4, Washington clinches its first-ever NLCS

TREATS

1988 Wrigley Field: this Cathedral's first night game on 8-8-88. "Let there be light(s)." The game rained out after four innings. First full game under the lights was on the next day—the Cubs beat the Mets (of course they did)

AFTER-FORWARD

1985–1988: Maxwell House Mug Nights, many teams, many stadiums, many mugs

2001 Shea Stadium: Yanks-Mets interleague game with my dad and sister

2010 Nationals Park: pitching phenom Stephen Strasburg home game debut, with the President politically rooting for both sides—the Nat rookie and his White Sox

2001, 2002, 2017, 2019—Edison Field (Anaheim), Turner Field (Atlanta), Citi Field, and Nationals Park—all business or family suites

2018 Nationals Park: All-Star week's Home Run Derby with grandson

2018 Nationals Park: watching NY Mets pitching ace Jacob DeGrom lock up his first Cy Young season with a win—and a season 1.70 ERA and 269 strikeouts—up close and personal with my grandson in seats on the dugout in late September

2019 Nationals Park: hosting a spring training game, not in AZ or FL but in DC, for local high school alumni and current students down from the Bronx vs. their favorite team of the Bronx

2019 Citi Field: September Mets game against Arizona to see the newly named *Tom Seaver Way* (126th Street) and Rookie of the Year, Polar Bear, Pete Alonso, delivering; bumping into a Mets cult hero at the hotel desk check-in

2021 Citi Field: Yanks/Mets Subway Series game on the 10th anniversary of 9/11, on 9/11, with my godson

2021 Nationals Park: attending first post-pandemic game in our seated pod

1965–2022 many other games

WORLD SERIES

1980 Royals Stadium: Kansas City Royals Game #4 (Win vs. Yanks)

1984 Tiger Stadium: Games # 3 and #4 (Win, Win vs. Padres)

1987 Busch Stadium: Game #4 Cards (Win vs. Giants)

2000 Shea Stadium: Game #5 Subway Series (Mets' end vs. the Yanks)

AFTER-FORWARD

The End*

*Though there does seem to be a lot more baseball to write about...

ACKNOWLEDGMENTS

Writing this last part should be as easy as dropping a bunt down the first base line. Except for, if you have watched baseball, especially over a long time, you know that it is not easy at all. It also is a lost art and a shame.

I do not know how writers of olden times who authored books that required factual history and accurate research did it—without access to the Internet. There must have been ways. Libraries, monasteries, royal or government records, academia, professional societies, and, I guess, those few with really, really good memories. I am glad that I live today, at least on this score.

I used the Internet regularly to fact check my memory and especially when it came down to the critical part: the numbers. At the start, I used a few baseball statistical websites. However, the singular source became baseball-reference.com. If it is not accurate, I probably am not, either.

Then there was the old-fashioned way. I read books, about 25, cover to cover, some hardcover, when I could find them. (I always liked a new one). All were entertaining and enlightening.

As far as the non-artificial intelligence side—AKA people—they were many. I've decided not to name them by name. If they made it this far or simply skipped ahead, they know who they are. I have grouped them in groups.

The Scouts: Early adopters, early on. I was fortunate to contact a small cadre of advisers. This was somewhat of a planned approach and, thankfully, a productive one. A few had authored books, fiction or nonfiction. All responded and went to bat for my idea—although they were more like umpires explaining an unwritten rule book.

Their sage sayings which stuck: writing the book is the easy part—the real work comes after; you have great stories, you should write a book—write it for your family; a successful sports author once said to me that the trick, at least for this sportswriter, was to write the way you speak; don't worry about how to publish it—write the damn thing first, and you'll figure out the other part later; you don't know how much you know until you write it all down—you know a lot about baseball. Finally, there was the ongoing feedback from a patient athletic director on his Virginia lake. He cheered me on and backed up my fielding.

The Fans: These can fill up a small baseball stadium or large neighborhood diamond: friends, neighbors, fellow school alumni, people who I had just met at Nationals Park or in a hotel bar, enthusiastic dads at Little

ACKNOWLEDGMENTS

League games, coworkers past and present, family near and far, the few who reviewed an early chapter draft or two, the many who I spoke to about my writing a baseball book, even just once, and even the non-baseball fan. Everyone listened and was genuinely interested. You know who you all are. Lastly, the professionals who helped me complete my pitching start. There was not one, single, solitary stitch of a negative vibe, anywhere, at any time. Quite the contrary. Give yourselves a standing ovation.

The Lineup: There would not be stories to recount, memories to recall, or facts to discuss decades later if it were not for the connections. Listed in order of their plate appearances: John Biltgen, Greg Price, Tony Aquilina, Declan Dickens, Bill Nolan, Mike Brown, Mike Myers, George Savage and Joe Talmage. Thank you, then and now.

The Instructional League: My elementary school (Christ the King in Yonkers, since closed down) where I learned arithmetic and how, in English class, to diagram sentences—the latter which, for some quirky reason, I greatly enjoyed (taken together, the two subjects vaguely resemble baseball in my mind's eye); Cardinal Hayes High School for its faculty and educational grounding, with its greatest experience being the rich diversity of my classmates—and an acquired appreciation of the full roster and a team effort; Manhattan College, which afforded me the chance to meet my wife, start a family, made me eligible for the college draft, and helped me land a job and begin a business career; Iona College, which taught me how to play night games and practice the discipline to multitask while you have a day job.

The Teams: My four employers with their customers, colleagues, and clients. Hall of Fame designation going to General Foods—the Maxwell House Division, that is—which paved the way for my lucky journey with baseball.

Home Field: Family, which is mostly what life is about—as well as a number of these chronicles. To have a loving, supportive family is more than a blessing, especially when it came to this labor of love. Their patience was a gift.

The Box Score: Thanks to our canine herd of Becky, Lola, and Mandy, always in the office with comforting licks of the ankles, calming requests for pets, or soulful eyes for this writer's reflection; for Daughter #2, Laura, rooting for my Mets and me; to Daughter #1, Cristina, who clearly explained to me what I was actually doing; to the grandkids with an All-Star selection for granddaughter #1, Carmen, already a creative writing award winner (before entering high school); to my wife, Maria, for putting up with me for much more than this obsession or for my love of baseball; to her parents who quickly saw me as their son; and to Valls, the only connection who regretfully isn't able to chronicle with me, but with whom I have watched the most games.

ACKNOWLEDGMENTS

To my brother, Bern, for his sense of humor and for seriously upgrading my baseball card collection. I miss you every day.

To Dad, for always being there and for seeing the glass half full, even when it might be empty. To Mom, for both her kindness toward everyone she met and her love of fun and life—how she will be forever remembered.

BIBLIOGRAPHY

Bouton, Jim, and Leonard Ed Shecter. *Ball Four; My Life and Hard Times Throwing the Knuckleball in the Big Leagues.* New York, World Pub. Co, 1970.

Burns, Ken, "Baseball | the Capital of Baseball | Episode 7." PBS, 1994 www.pbs.org/video/part-7-the-capital-of-baseball-96qtrl/.

Coffey, Wayne R. *They Said It Couldn't Be Done : The '69 Mets, New York City, and the Most Astounding Season in Baseball History.* New York, Crown Archetype, 2019.

Delillo, Don. *Pafko at the Wall : A Novella.* New York, Scribner, 2001.

Dickson, Paul. *LEO DUROCHER : Baseball's Prodigal Son.* New York/London, Bloomsbury, 2018.

Gordon, Devin. *So Many Ways to Lose : The Amazin' True Story of the New York Mets, the Best Worst Team in Sports.* New York, Ny, Harper, 2021.

Kahn, Roger. *The Boys of Summer*. London, Aurum, 2013.

Kaplan, Jim. *The Greatest Game Ever Pitched: Juan Marichal and Warren Spahn and the Pitching Duel of the Century,* Chicago, IL, Triumph Books 2001.

LIEBOWITZ), John Drebinger the *New York Times* (BY MEYER. "SOME of BIG GUNS in DODGERS' ANSWERING SALVO; Dodgers Win, Tie Play-Offs as Labine Halts Giants, 10-0 Edge Conceded to Giants DODGERS WIN, 10-0, and TIE PLAY-OFFS Thirtieth Homer for Pafko Lights Turned on for Sixth Robinson Hits First Pitch Umpire Wins Another Argument." *The New York Times*, 3 Oct. 1951, www.nytimes.com/1951/10/03/archives/some-of-big-guns-in-dodgers-answering-salvo-dodgers-win-tie.html.

Madden, Bill. *1954 : The Year Willie Mays and the First Generation of Black Superstars Changed Major League Baseball Forever*. Boston, Ma, Da Capo Press, A Member of Perseus Books Group, 2015.

Madden, Bill. *Tom Seaver : A Terrific Life*. New York, Simon & Schuster, 2020.

"Monologue: George Carlin on Football and Baseball - SNL." *YouTube*, Oct. 24, 2013, www.youtube.com/watch?v=5ebyLkCaAL0

"October 4, 1951." *Archive.nytimes.com*, 4 Oct. 1951, archive.nytimes.com/www.nytimes.com/books/97/10/05/home/frontpage.html. Accessed 14 June 2022.

"Piazza Leads Mets in First Sporting Event after 9/11." *YouTube*, 17 Apr. 2020, www.youtube.com/watch?v=VVEHuRnJbSU.

Posnanski, Joe. *The Baseball 100*. New York, Ny, Avid Reader Press, An Imprint Of Simon & Schuster, Inc, 2021.

Prager, Joshua. *The Echoing Green : The Untold Story of Bobby Thomson, Ralph Branca, and the Shot Heard Round the World*. New York, Vintage Books, 2008.

Rapoport, Ron. *Let's Play Two : The Legend of Mr. Cub, the Life of Ernie Banks*. New York, Hachette Books, 2020.